ABOUT THE AUTHORS

CHIP CONLEY is founder and president of Joie de Vivre America, a San Francisco–based hotel management company. Previously Chip was a partner with Bay West Development Company, where he was instrumental in some of the West Coast's largest building renovation projects. He has both an M.B.A. and a B.A. from Stanford University. Chip writes screenplays in his rather limited spare time.

SETH GODIN is founder of The Skeibo Press, Inc., a publisher of guides and directories. He is also a successful direct-mail consultant, and has created and marketed more than fifty video and software products with Spinnaker Software. Seth has a degree in computer engineering from Tufts University, and received his M.B.A. from Stanford. Seth and his wife, Helene, live in Mt. Vernon, New York.

D0959143

"BUSINESS RULES OF THUMB"

Seth Godin
and
Chip Conley

WARNER BOOKS

A Warner Communications Company

This book is dedicated to our parents.

Copyright © 1987 by Seth Godin and Chip Conley
All rights reserved.
Warner Books, Inc., 666 Fifth Avenue, New York, NY 10103

W A Warner Communications Company

Book Design by Nick Mazzella

Printed in the United States of America
First Printing: July 1987
10 9 8 7 6 5 4 3 2 1

Library of Congress Cataloging-in-Publication Data
 Godin, Seth.
  Business rules of thumb.

  Includes index.
  1. Success in business. I. Conley, Chip. II. Title.
HF5386.G55 1987   650.1   87-6262
ISBN 0-446-37026-6 (U.S.A.)
ISBN 0-446-37027-4 (Can.)

Contents

Preface

Ability is the art of getting credit for all the home runs somebody else hits.

Casey Stengel

This book is a compilation of home runs (with a few strikeouts thrown in to keep you on your toes): business rules, tips, and wisdoms passed on through the ages and cataloged for the first time.

Business Rules of Thumb is a by-product of a research project in decision making begun at the Stanford Graduate School of Business in 1983. Through interviews with hundreds of business leaders, our project focused on the methods and means by which executives make business decisions. We immediately discovered that, faced with a multitude of various business dilemmas daily, executive decision makers use their intuition or past experiences as the chief influence in their decision making. Personal rules of thumb were the overwhelmingly favorite instrument used by these executives in navigating through business life.

WHAT IS A THUMB?

We define a rule of thumb as a short (less than a paragraph in length) instruction for dealing with a set of circumstances.

Rules of thumb often serve as important shortcuts, allowing the user to make a decision with less time and less information than he or she might desire.

Some rules stand the test of time, some don't. Thirty years ago, American real estate developers lived by the rule "Don't build a building unless you have a tenant already committed to the space." Trammell Crow, the largest real estate developer in America today, was one of the first to challenge this rule. His success in building industrial warehouses in anticipation of demand, rather than in reaction to it, significantly diminished the credibility of that rule (although it is once again coming into vogue). On the other hand, some rules of thumb may last forever. For example, "Advertisements with people in them get better results than those without."

A DOUBLE-EDGED SWORD

The rule of thumb offers the user a powerful benefit, yet it also carries a powerful drawback. In every industry and every job we examined, rules are used constantly. They allow the decision maker to make decisions more quickly and with less information than they otherwise could. In fact, one of the key differences between an "experienced" and an "inexperienced" employee is knowledge of an industry's rules.

These rules tend to be passed on from employee to employee and learned over time. Once used, the rules become second nature to the employee, and their validity is taken for granted.

The danger, of course, is in the indiscriminate use of these rules. Because it is easy to learn the rule and not its basis in fact, the rules often replace reason. The rules become a crutch, and in some cases completely replace independent decision making (the insurance adjuster is perhaps our favorite example).

It's not hard to think of dozens of examples of middle managers in paralysis, unable to bend because a given situation contradicts an existing rule of thumb. More surprising is how widespread "thumb paralysis" seems to be: marketing vice-presidents that use rules to set pricing and design advertising, CEOs that establish personnel policies based only on rules, presidents and premiers that negotiate the future of the world with them.

We hope that you'll find these rules valuable, or at least entertaining. Our graduates from the "school of hard knocks" range from Fortune 500 chief executives to starving artists, and the subjects range from building character to building a house.

The Rule of Thumb Hall of Fame

Throughout the book, we've included information about individuals and organizations that we consider worthy of inclusion in the Rule of Thumb Hall of Fame. These men, women, and organizations are highlighted for popularizing business maxims, paradigms, and rules. The books and articles written by these Hall of Famers have been internationally acclaimed, and have combined to sell over half a billion copies.

A Universal Rule of Thumb

A rule brought to us by L. J. Urbano states that virtually all authors end their prefaces with "and thanks to my wife and kids, who were patient throughout the creation of this manuscript." (Go ahead—check.)

The authors are indebted to two publications for the wealth of materials and insight that they provide on Rules of Thumb. We highly recommend *Boardroom Reports*, a bi-weekly newsletter, and *Rules of Thumb*, by Tom Parker, published by Harper & Row.

This book was invented at a regular weekly meeting of the Stanford Entrepreneurial Roundtable. All of the other members, Evan Schlesinger, Ed Zimbler, and John Gonzales, made important contributions. At the GSB, Associate Dean Eugene Webb provided invaluable assistance, as did all of the professors who contributed rules. Special thanks go to Professor Dave Jemison, to whom one of the authors still owes a paper.

We received assistance from BayWest Development and Spinnaker Software, as well as from our editor at Warner, Jim Frost. And of course, thanks to Seth's wife, Helene, for putting up with all of this, and more. (Far be it from us to violate a rule of thumb!)

1
TOUGH AS NAILS
Negotiating

CLIFF MILLER
Real Estate Leasing Agent
Royal LePage

In negotiating over a period of time with a committee, use their sheer numbers against them. Focus on the contradictions which various members have expressed.

CHARLES KARRASS
Author
Give and Take

Guidelines for preparing a negotiating-meeting agenda:

a. Don't accept the other man's agenda without thinking through the consequences.
b. Consider where and how issues can best be introduced.
c. Schedule the discussion of issues to give yourself time to think.
d. Study the opponent's proposed agenda for what it deliberately leaves out.

ANONYMOUS

In a negotiation, he who cares less, wins.

CHARLES KARRASS

Do not make a last and final offer until you have evaluated precisely how the statement will be made and how discussions will be continued if it is not honored.

ARTURO JIMENEZ
Weight Trainer

Your body weight
    divided by
combined body weight of you and your negotiating opponent
    equals
Percent of time you will win a negotiation with this opponent.

CHARLES KARRASS

Don't go into a negotiation without listing every issue beforehand. Establish an aspiration level, a minimum, and an initial asking price for each issue.

MARVIN LEVIN
Co-founder
Consolidated Capital Companies

If you're planning on doing business with someone again, don't be too tough in the negotiations. If you're going to skin a cat don't keep it as a housecat.

GEORGE DEUKMEJIAN
Governor
State of California

Don't get caught focusing on the cents, and not the dollars, in a negotiation.

MARK McCORMACK
Author
What They Don't Teach You at Harvard Business School

If you don't like what you're hearing, respond with a question, even if it's no more than "Why are you saying that?"

Business Rules of Thumb
HALL OF FAME

MARK H. McCORMACK—Mr. McCormack, named by *Sports Illustrated* as "the most powerful man in sports," is the chairman of IMG, a sports consulting, merchandising, and management company. The company represents such diverse events and entities as Wimbledon, the NFL, and the Nobel Foundation. Mr. McCormack's book *What They Don't Teach You at Harvard Business School* was a national best-seller.

GERALD I. NIERENBERG
Author
The Art of Negotiation

In preparing for negotiations with another person, carefully investigate any deals he has failed to conclude successfully. If you carefully analyze the reasons that a certain deal fell through or a negotiation failed, you will probably get a good understanding of how the opponent thinks, his method of operating, and his psychological approach.

JEFF FURMAN
Business Consultant

If you are negotiating for money, pay careful attention to the increments of change in your opponent's demands. When the increments begin to decrease in size, your opponent is reaching his or her bargaining limit.

CATHLEEN BONE
Educator

Always wear a facial bandage or two into an initial negotiating meeting.

GERALD I. NIERENBERG

When a negotiation appears to be headed toward an impasse, it is a good strategy to clear the air by a flat statement such as, "It's the best we can do under the circumstances."

EDWIN SILBERSTANG
Games Expert

There are three factors involved in successful bluffing:

1. Your opponent: it is easier to bluff a strong player than a weak one.
2. Your position in the game: it is easier to bluff a big loser than a big winner.
3. Money: the bigger the stakes, the easier it is to bluff.

Don't bluff unless you have at least two of these factors on your side.

S. T. CONLEY, SR.
President
Bancap Investment Group

In negotiating, never be the first to name a price.

GERALD I. NIERENBERG

The rate of a person's blinking is higher when the person is angry or excited.

JAY M. KAPLAN
Former President
Consolidated Capital Companies

Talk about price last. People have tremendous anxieties about hearing the price, so use preliminary negotiations to get all the auxiliary issues resolved first. Say "If the price is OK, would you be willing to . . ."

EUGENE WEBB
Associate Dean
Stanford Graduate School of Business

Only negotiate with people who have less than half the access to capital resources that you do.

CHIP CONLEY

In preparing for a negotiation, pick three specific definable goals which you plan to achieve and don't walk away from the table until you accomplish these goals.

HENRY FORD
Founder
Ford Motor Co.

The most powerful seat at the negotiating table is at the head of the table.

JEFFREY STILING
Systems Engineer
IBM

When you are in a negotiation session with someone else who has strict time deadlines for the meeting, defer many of the important decisions until the end of the meeting, as your opponent will likely be more malleable then.

MARK McCORMACK

Round numbers beg to be negotiated, usually by counteroffer round numbers. Odd numbers sound harder, firmer, less negotiable.

JON Q. REYNOLDS
President
Reynolds and Brown

He who controls time controls the negotiation.

JONATHON VISBAL
International Business Strategist
Pacific Telesis International

Role-play a negotiation with an associate at least twice before getting in the "ring" with your opponent.

CAROLYN REECE
Accountant

Always outnumber your opponent with bodies at the negotiating table.

MARK MCCORMACK

One party generally benefits more than the other from vague or nonbinding language in a contract or letter agreement. Determine up front whether a vague agreement or an airtight one better suits your purpose.

SETH GODIN

In general, the party with the least resources benefits most from an airtight agreement.

CHIP CONLEY

As a buyer approaching a negotiating meeting, be sure to trumpet any bad economic news headlines as much as possible.

GERALD I. NIERENBERG

When two groups are negotiating at a conference table, try to sit on the side of the table with the opposing group. Then, attempt to take issue with certain propositions proposed by your group, siding with the opposition. In minor disputes this appears to work, because the opposition begins to consider you as a member of their team. Thereafter, they will listen most agreeably to your proposals for solving the points of disagreement.

KARL VESPER
Author and Consultant

The more a negotiator knows about what he or she is attempting to buy, the better the negotiating position.

——— Business Rules of Thumb ———
——— HALL OF FAME ———

KARL H. VESPER—Mr. Vesper is a well-known consultant, author, and corporate board member. As a professor of business at the University of Washington, Mr. Vesper is best known for his research on entrepreneuring.

MARIAN McCONNELL
Corporate Strategist
Turner Broadcasting Co.

Start a negotiation with easy issues rather than complex ones.

MARK RANDALL
Sports Consultant

Throw a temper tantrum within the first ten minutes of the negotiating—nine out of ten times it will effectively intimidate your opponent.

PHILIP SPERBER
Author
The Science of Business Negotiations

Always push to hold the early negotiating sessions at the opponent's office. The side on its home turf has the advantage. If the opponent hosts the first meetings, there's strong justification for moving the later, more crucial sessions away from its place.

GERALD I. NIERENBERG

In negotiations, always deal with the principal, not the agent.

SETH GODIN

The best advantage is gained if you can have your agent deal with their principal. This gives you the flexibility of making decisions outside the negotiation, while you can hold the other side to all concessions made.

SY BALIN
Management Consultant

In approaching a negotiation, if you are the seller, build a 20 percent optimistic factor into the value of the item you're selling, and, if you're the buyer, build a 20 percent pessimistic factor into its value.

ROBERT ALLEN
Real Estate Investor, Writer, and Seminar Entrepreneur

When negotiating a dollar-amount settlement, think of cash as the most precious commodity in the world—one which is severely limited.

ROBERT OLSON
Fashion Model and Actor

Successful negotiations are 70 percent preparation, 20 percent implementation, and 10 percent acting.

RONALD W. REAGAN
President
United States of America

Always negotiate from a position of strength.

GERALD I. NIERENBERG

In questioning your negotiating opponent, you should give him a plan in advance of what you intend to gain from the conversation.

LLOYD ALLWOOD
Labor Attorney

Always surprise your opponent with your initial demand.

LLOYD ALLWOOD

Prior to the negotiation, have a list of ten issues which weaken your opponent's argument and have a list of ten rebuttals to expected objections from your opponent.

ALEXANDER SEBASTIAN
International Business Consultant

Do not assume that your opponent knows your weaknesses.

VICTOR ANTONETTI
Starving Artist

Never negotiate on a full stomach.

ROBERT RINGER
Author
Winning Through Intimidation

The results a person obtains are inversely proportional to the degree to which the person is intimidated.

2
HEY, KID, WANNA BE A <u>MILLION</u>AIRE?
Starting a New Business

GREG ANRIG, JR.
Money Magazine

If you are enamored of an idea for a product and want to reduce the risk and up-front cost, hire a separate firm to make it while you act as a licensing agent in selling it to retailers.

STEVEN BRANDT
Author and Professor
Stanford Graduate Business School

TEN COMMANDMENTS FOR A NEW BUSINESS

1. Limit the number of primary participants to people who can consciously agree upon and contribute directly to that which the enterprise is to accomplish, for whom, and by when.
2. Define the business of the enterprise in terms of what is to be bought, precisely by whom, and why.
3. Concentrate all available resources on accomplishing

12

two or three specific, operational objectives within a given time period.

4. Prepare and work from a written plan that delineates who in the total organization is to do what, by when.

5. Employ key people with proven records of success at doing what needs to be done in a manner consistent with the desired value system of the enterprise.

6. Reward individual performance that exceeds agreed-upon standards.

7. Expand methodically from a profitable base toward a balanced business.

8. Project, monitor, and conserve cash and credit capability.

9. Maintain a detached point of view.

10. Anticipate incessant change by periodically testing adopted business plans for consistency with the realities of the world marketplace.

Business Rules of Thumb
HALL OF FAME

STEVEN C. BRANDT—Mr. Brandt has been the president of four high-growth companies, most recently, the Cdex Corporation. He has been on the faculty of the Stanford Graduate School of Business since 1971 and authored *Entrepreneuring*, one of the landmark books on starting a new business.

ROBERT KESSLER
Principal
Custom Sample Systems

The less time and money it takes to start and manage a company, the more likely it is to succeed. First-time entrepreneurs are better off pursuing ideas they can implement handily.

ALAIN BAPTISTE
Entrepreneur

To figure out what market niches exist for new businesses in your community, get the Yellow Pages of a similar community and compare them to your community's Yellow Pages. Notice what products or services are missing.

BIRGE M. CLARK
Partner
Clark, Stromquist & Sandstrom

In starting a new business, try to locate in a small or medium-size community so that your reputation can build quickly.

FREDERICK ADLER
Senior Partner
Reavis & McGrath

TEN RULES OF VENTURE CAPITAL

The probability that a company will succeed is inversely proportional to the amount of publicity received before it began to manufacture its first product.

An investor's ability to talk about winners is an order of magnitude greater than the ability to remember the losers.

If a venture capital investor does not think he has a problem, he has a big problem.

Happiness is positive cash flow. Everything else will come later.

The probability of a small firm's success is inversely proportional to the president's office size.

Would-be entrepreneurs who pick up the check after luncheon discussions are usually losers.

The longer the investment proposal, the shorter the odds of success.

There is no such thing as an overfinanced company.

Managers who worry a lot about voting control usually have nothing worth controlling.

There is no limit on what a person can do or where he can go if he does not mind who gets credit.

CHASE REVEL
Entrepreneur

Don't use your personal name as part of the business name of a new company, as this protects you in case the company fails and protects you against disagreeable business practices of a future purchaser.

DAVID HOLLAS
Author
The Making of an Entrepreneur

The first person to hire when you go into business should be a good bookkeeper.

JOAN KELLY
Entrepreneur

Before going into a partnership with someone, spend time with them in three different kinds of situations: a relaxing one, a competitive one, and an intellectually stimulating one.

HERBERT M. DWIGHT, JR.
President
Spectra-Physics, Inc.

Before starting your own business, obtain at least five years of solid line operating experience in a large, well-managed company with well-developed training programs, or in a small company environment that challenges the limits of one's abilities.

JAMES G. TREYBIG
President
Tandem Computers

Choose carefully your first people in starting a business. Make sure they have quality as humans, that they are more qualified than yourself, and that at least one has already been successful.

SANDRA KURTZIG
Founder
Ask Computers

When starting a new company, don't rush to assemble a Board of Directors—instead, start out with a Board of Advisors, as they will appreciate the limited liability.

JAY CONRAD LEVINSON
Author
Guerrilla Marketing

If you start five earning endeavors, it is likely three will fail.

KENICHI OHMAE
Author
The Mind of the Strategist

The idea for a new venture is likely to be strategically unsound if it can't be put into one coherent sentence.

KENNETH G. SLETTON
Executive Vice-president
Rudolph & Sletton General Contractors

In starting a new business, establish a company philosophy and revise it as the company grows so that everyone in the company can buy into and be a part of the overall objectives.

LINDA H. SCHATZ
Vice-president
Partners on Purpose

Very early in the process of starting a new company, establish a board of overseers, a few trusted friends and colleagues you meet with regularly and report to.

CHIP CONLEY

Don't go into partnership with anyone you've known less than one year, unless they're putting up all the money.

MARK McCORMACK
Author
What They Don't Teach You at Harvard Business School

When projecting overhead for your new venture, make an estimate of your annual overhead and then, for purposes of planning, double it.

NICHOLAS J. DINAPOLI
Director of Engineering
Pneu Devices, Inc.

Prepare a business plan that will allow you to exist at the bare survival level. Don't focus on growth.

BILL EDWARDS
President
Bryan & Edwards

The key elements for a successful new venture:

- **a.** experienced management team
- **b.** potential for becoming a significant company
- **c.** technical excellence
- **d.** sound, sensible business plan
- **e.** focused strategy
- **f.** sense of urgency

PROFESSOR ARNOLD COOPER and WILLIAM DUNKULBERG
Purdue University

The chances of success of a new company are generally greater with two full-time partners rather than a solo entrepreneur.

RICHARD M. WHITE
Author
The Entrepreneur's Manual

HOW VENTURE CAPITALISTS EVALUATE A START-UP

—LOCAL RETAIL SALES OR RETAIL SERVICE

Management team	30–50% of the importance
Location	40–50%
Products/Services	5–10%
Mktng/Finance plans	1–5%

—NATIONWIDE INDUSTRIAL BUSINESS

Management team	60–90% of the importance
Key employees	10–30%
Industry	10–20%
The service	10–15%
Mktng/Finance plans	1–5%

—MANUFACTURING

Management team	50–60% of the importance
Industry	20–30%
Product	10–20%
Mktng/Finance plans	5–10%

ROBERT McKIM
Professor
Stanford University

Fear engenders conformity and is a powerful barrier to creativity. If you are an entrepreneur, analyze your obsessive motivations for starting a business and attempt to reduce the importance of the fear of failure as one of the motivating influences on your career.

ROBERT TILLMAN
Director of Marketing
Paradise Systems

When recruiting a management team for a new company, the president should always be hired first and should hire his own team.

NICHOLAS J. DINAPOLI

Don't conduct your start-up planning in a closet. Talk to your potential competitors, customers, and suppliers. Be reasonably free with information regarding your plans, and you will get a wealth of useful information in return.

STANLEY RICH and DAVID GUMPERT
Authors
Business Plans That Win $$$

Venture capitalists are typically looking to liquidate small company investments three to seven years down the road at a return of 35 to 60 percent annually.

ROBERT TILLMAN

A start-up company should never be in more than one market.

RICHARD M. WHITE

Venture capitalists expect to make five to seven times their money in five years.

STANLEY RICH and DAVID GUMPERT

In a successful business plan, investors look for:
1. Evidence of consumer acceptance
2. Appreciation of investor needs
3. Evidence of focus
4. Proprietary position

RICHARD M. WHITE

In manufacturing and major service start-ups, the combined salaries of the marketing and sales groups should not exceed 5 percent of net sales after the fourth year.

STEWART BRAND
Founder
Whole Earth Catalog

Start cheap, small, and local. That keeps your mistakes survivable and your customer feedback loops rapid and accurate.

RICHARD M. WHITE

Many start-ups pay their founders 20 percent of the net profit (before taxes) instead of salaries.

WILLIAM LATTIN
Director of Engineering
OMNET Associates

Hire new employees for your business to complement your weaknesses, and hire them only when you can truly make a long-term commitment to them.

STANLEY RICH and DAVID GUMPERT

Four turnoffs in business plans:

1. Product orientation
2. Projections which deviate excessively from industry norms
3. Unrealistic growth projections
4. Custom or applications engineering approaches

RICHARD M. WHITE

The more successful a start-up is, the greater will be its need for larger and more frequent cash injections.

3
BIG MAC TO MACINTOSH
New-Product Development

TOM PETERS and BOB WATERMAN
Authors
In Search of Excellence

An engineering and R&D staff should give priority to making and adjusting the prototype and less emphasis to getting the specs down on paper. Do the drawings when you have a finished product.

SETH GODIN

The two worst things to say to a creative person:

1. That's been done before.
2. That's never been done before.

ALLAN MICHAELS
CEO
Convergent Technologies

No new internal venture/product team should ever have more than three people on it initially.

NICHOLAS J. DINAPOLI
Director of Engineering
Pneu Devices, Inc.

In bringing a new product to the market, it is essential for you to know the difference between a marketable product and a fascinating research project (with market potential). Your ability to make that determination is likely to be the difference between success and failure.

DUVALL Y. HECHT
Founder
Independent Securities Corp.

Make sure the central idea is correct. If it is, it will have sufficient vitality to allow you time to work out the details. The inverse of this proposition is not true—the details will not save a flawed central idea.

CHESTER R. WASSON
Author
Dynamic Competitive Strategy and Product Life Cycles

During the introductory period of a new product, use exclusive and selective means of distribution so that the distribution margins are high enough to justify heavy promotional spending.

EUGENE FINKIN
Senior Consultant
Westinghouse Corp.

Achieving meaningful profits from new-product research and development usually takes between seven and eleven years from the inception of a program.

SETH GODIN

People don't steal ideas. Ideas are cheap. Implementation makes the difference.

TOM PETERS and BOB WATERMAN

To promote the success of a company's new-products division, locate the engineering and R&D departments next to each other in order to facilitate communication.

GEORGE BALLAS
Inventor
Weedeater

It takes a large company normally eighteen months to do the concept and product development phase of a new idea or product.

INSIDE R&D

Bring a bright idea into focus quickly by assigning a high-level executive sponsor to it. To carry a new product through its early stages, don't rely on part-time contributions from workers with other duties. Put on a full-time team.

KARL VESPER
Author and Professor of Entrepreneurship

A new product should have at least three different substantial advantages over its competitors in order to justify support.

PROCTER & GAMBLE

When introducing a new food product, require that consumers prefer its taste two to one over the chief competitor.

RONALD B. NEWHOUSE III
Management Consultant

Companies who spend 10 percent more than their competitors on research and development have twice the success rate in new-product introductions.

ROBERT TOWNSEND
Former President, Avis Rent-A-Car
Author, Up the Organization

Don't start raving about a new idea to everyone in the corporation. Instead, enlist the support of those who like the idea, think it through, then propose it.

SETH GODIN

In choosing the name of a new product or service, there are only two guidelines that must be met (all other guidelines are superfluous): a) Flexibility: Does the name transcend price categorization? Is it sufficiently broad enough to allow changes in the product/service? b) Pleasant-sounding: Is the name easy to say and hear? Does the sound of the name get the point across?

THOMAS POOLE
Marketing Times

Thirty percent of new-product failures had a concept that met no clear need.

HERBERT M. DWIGHT, JR.
President
Spectra-Physics, Inc.

Select a business with a product line that is technically unique and difficult to copy and whose characteristics ensure an expanding market niche of reasonable size.

JOEL DEAN

The promotional expenditures [for a new product] will tend to pay for themselves many times over in the form of sales. A high initial price will allow for a large advertising allowance.

GEORGE BALLAS and DAVID HOLLAS
Authors
Making of an Entrepreneur

RULES FOR A SUCCESSFUL INNOVATION

1. Relative advantage over existing products.
2. Must be compatible with existing attitudes and beliefs.
3. It shouldn't be complex.
4. Benefits of the innovation must be easily communicable.
5. The innovation should be divisible—users can try the innovation without incurring a large risk.
6. Buyer must believe that the innovation satisfies one of his needs by giving some immediate benefit.

4
WHAT'S A QUICHE NICHE?
Marketing

GERALD M. KATZ
Pricing Specialist

Don't destroy the long-run "positioning" of a product in the market by excessive price cutting. If you have a premium product, constant price cutting may "cheapen the image" and hurt sales over time. But occasional discounting may tempt new customers to try the product and become regular buyers.

ALAN AMSLER
Graphic Designer

You should figure that layout and finished art for a high-quality brochure will cost you $250 per page.

BOARDROOM REPORTS

Print "preferred customer" on direct-mail solicitations, invoices, and other standard forms. To maintain effectiveness, every six months, change the wording to alert the customer of his special status.

BUSINESS MAILER QUARTERLY

Best months for business mail-order campaigns: January, February, September, and October.

DR. HAROLD W. FOX
Professor
Ball State University

Consider setting price above rivals when:

- Customers easily pass their costs forward or they regularly sell on a cost-plus basis
- The item accounts for only a small fraction of the buyer's total costs
- The product is so integrated into customers' systems that switching would be either expensive or inconvenient
- Buyers' engineers or plant managers are more influential than the purchasing department

JAY CONRAD LEVINSON
Author
Guerrilla Marketing

The most important qualities in a marketing executive are: patience, imagination, ego-strength, and aggressiveness.

ANA and JOHN KADON
Authors
Successful Public Relations Techniques

Never send a letter addressed OCCUPANT or RESIDENT.

L. PERRY WILBUR
Author
Money in Your Mailbox

You're not ready to publish your own mail-order catalog until you have at least ten thousand customers.

MAIL ORDER DIGEST

Phone marketing achieves the best results on Mondays and Tuesdays. December and January are the best months.

OPINION RESEARCH CORP.

Sixty-five percent of those using coupons use them for products they normally buy anyway.

JULIAN SIMON
Author
Getting into the Mail-Order Business

HOW TO SUCCEED IN MAIL ORDER

1. Do what is being done successfully.
2. Never innovate, never offer really new products.
3. Offer your product in a similar manner and in exactly the same media as the innovator.

RICHARD M. WHITE
Author
The Entrepreneur's Manual

In high-tech companies, selling expenses (commissions, salaries, travel, advertising, literature) are usually 10 to 30 percent of the net sales after the fourth year. In most low-tech companies, these percentages increase to 25 to 40 percent of net sales. In franchises, usually the percentages are down around 1 to 3 percent. Retail operations generally run to the 10 to 15 percent range.

EDWARD MEYER
Director of Promotion Services
Dancer, Fitzgerald, Sample

Cost to put a sample of a new consumer product in the hands of one thousand people:

- Mail: $88
- Hanging on doorknob: $160
- Handing out on street corner: up to $70

LEONARD PACE
Management Consultant
Deloitte, Haskins & Sells

During a weakening of the economy, if sales of branded items are off, look into special promotions, under a new name, to a new audience. For example, a food item that normally sells to consumers could be packaged and sold to the institutional market on a promotional basis to keep production going.

JAY CONRAD LEVINSON

Once you develop a marketing plan, stick with the strategy for at least one year.

EXHIBITS SURVEY, INC.

A trade show visitor will stop at about twenty booths per trade show. The average stop lasts about fifteen minutes, so keep your demonstrations to less than ten minutes to allow for conversation.

DR. HAROLD W. FOX

It's advantageous to keep prices below the competition's when:

- The company is expanding into a new market
- The product has a high proportion of fixed costs to the value-added
- The company has idle capacity
- It is desirable to expand production to gain economies of scale

JAY CONRAD LEVINSON

Your marketing message should be written and presented so that it appeals to both left- and right-brain thinkers.

Business Rules of Thumb
HALL OF FAME

JAY CONRAD LEVINSON—Mr. Levinson, in his many books, espouses the principle of "earning money without a job (or more appropriately, amassing a fortune by initiating simultaneous business ventures)." His books *Guerrilla Marketing* and *Earning Money Without a Job* have earned Mr. Levinson a reputation as a leader in unconventional business wisdom.

CUSTOMER SERVICE IN ACTION

Offer customers a guarantee on an aspect of the business that is routinely performed.

BOARDROOM REPORTS

Coupons generate new-product trials at lowest cost, win high initial market share quickly, and have greatest appeal during recessions when consumers are looking for bargains.

SHELL ALPERT

Real stamps instead of metered inkblots raise the response rate of mailing to consumers at home.

A. C. NEILSEN & CO.

At least ten months are needed on average before a manufacturer can be reasonably certain of a new product's market share.

JACK FALVEY
Management Consultant

Marketing supports sales. Not vice versa.

PATRICIA WALTON
Marketing Representative
IBM

USEFUL DIRECT MAIL TIPS

BEST DAYS: Tuesday and Wednesday are the best days for your mail to reach your prospects.

BEST MONTHS: October, January, February, September, March, April, November, December, May, June, August, July—in that order, your mailings will elicit the most to the least response.

5
"WOULD YOU LIKE IT IN BLUE OR RED?"
Sales Techniques and Management

AMACOM
The Skills of Selling

When fielding questions from a customer, paraphrase his objections, avoid showing resistance, and question him tactfully on those parts of his arguments that seem to be weak.

DALE CARNEGIE
Noted Author and Philosopher

With a shrewd buyer, ask them for their advice on the product rather than trying to sell it to them.

───── Business Rules of Thumb ─────
───── HALL OF FAME ─────

DALE CARNEGIE—Best known for his book *How to Win Friends and Influence People*, Mr. Carnegie gained international fame for his teachings on self-motivation and interpersonal relations. His educational organization has continued to flourish and is now located in over one thousand cities across the United States and fifty countries abroad.

DAVID D. SELTZ
Author
How to Conduct Successful Sales Contests and Incentive Programs

A well-conceived sales contest should set a quota based on the individual's percentage improvement over past performance.

JOHN M. TRUTTEN
Author
Salesmanship: Ten Steps for Boosting Your Sales Right Now

Involve salespeople in setting sales quotas.

KENNETH A. MEYERS
President
Golightly & Co. International

Don't present the service or product until the prospective customer's objectives are completely understood.

LUTHER BROCK
Author
Direct Marketing

MAKE SALES LETTERS MORE EFFECTIVE

- Put the biggest enticement in the headline or first sentence.
- Add a postscript to attract additional attention.
- Be repetitive.
- Don't overuse underscores, notes in margins, and other such devices. (The higher the income of the audience, the less effective such tricks become.)

MARK McCORMACK
Author
What They Don't Teach You at Harvard Business School

If you're only there to sell one thing, make a suggestion or assumption and let them tell you you're wrong. People have a need to feel smarter than you are.

McGRAW-HILL RESEARCH

The average sales call costs $205.40

KENNETH A. MEYERS

Make sure the initial sales call includes at least one request by either the salesperson or the customer for a small favor.

MELL HOLLOWAY
Stockbroker

Sprinkle your sales letters or presentations with references to your subject's first name.

MIREK SPRINGER
German Actor

Offer your customer a choice between two alternatives; don't force the customer into a "yes/no" decision on one alternative.

RICHARD M. WHITE
Author
The Entrepreneur's Manual

Salesmen tend to sell what sells easily and they tend to be interested in gross sales, not net profits.

HARVARD BUSINESS REVIEW

LADDER OF COMMUNICATION EFFECTIVENESS (FROM LEAST EFFECTIVE TO MOST EFFECTIVE)

- Handout
- Advertisement
- News item
- Brochure
- Newsletter
- Mass-produced letter

- Typewritten letter
- Handwritten letter
- Telephone conversation
- Large group discussion
- Small group discussion
- One-to-one conversation

ROBERT TILLMAN
Director of Marketing
Paradise Systems, Inc.

Never sign an exclusive territorial contract with a manufacturer's rep firm with more than a thirty-day termination clause.

SALESMAKERS SYNDICATED SERVICES

Summer sales calls should be scheduled in the middle of the week to avoid prospects who are taking long weekends.

UNITED RESEARCH CORP.

Salespeople using computers gain 15 percent more selling time.

THE PROFESSIONAL REPORT

Contract with an independent sales agent, rather than hiring new staff salespeople, if:

A. A new product is aimed at markets outside the company's established channels of distribution.
B. A territory's potential volume is small.
C. Customer orders are infrequent, and sales are volatile.

HENNY YOUNGMAN
Comedian

Send telegrams. Everyone opens telegrams.

RUSS JOHNSON
Former Real Estate Sales Manager
Ashwill-Burke, Inc.

Make sure your sales staff is equally weighted with "wise veterans" and "Young Turks," as they tend to learn from each other.

RICHARD M. WHITE

The average rep firm spends from $300 to $500 per manufacturing principal per salesman per month.

RICHARD C. SMYTH and MATTHE J. MURPHEY
Compensating and Motivating Salesmen

It's best to introduce new sales incentive plans during good times because the sales force will be quickly convinced of its value when they reap immediate benefits. Incentive plans introduced during recessions usually turn out to be too generous to the salespeople when good times return.

MICHAEL MAKINNEY
Door-to-Door Salesman

Salespeople should brush their teeth and gargle with mouthwash at least three times during the workday.

McGRAW-HILL RESEARCH
Computer + Software News

Sales reps spend 32 percent of their time on waiting and travel, 24 percent on administration and meetings, 5 percent on service calls, and only 39 percent of their time selling.

MARK McCORMACK

Make sales presentations one-to-one to the key decision maker. Try to restrict it to one person because this does not allow the dynamics of the interrelationships of the individuals to affect the presentation.

LEE IACOCCA
Chairman of the Board
Chrysler Corporation

Never go before your customers without rehearsing what you want to say—as well as what you're going to do—to help sell your product.

KENNETH A. MEYERS

Never begin a sales call with a presentation.

MARK McCORMACK

Once you get to the point in a sales pitch where you have asked for a commitment, don't speak again until the other person has replied in some fashion.

KENNETH A. MEYERS

Request only fifteen minutes of the prospective customer's time on the first appointment. Be prepared to leave when the fifteen minutes are up.

JANUZ DIRECT MARKETING LETTER

Telephone salespeople should always let the customer hang up first.

DALE CARNEGIE

Smile.

ANDREW KEATON
National Sales Manager
The Dietzgen Corporation

Salespeople should talk only 20 percent of the time during their first visit with a potential customer and listen the other 80 percent.

AGENCY SALES MAGAZINE

When selling to a committee, zero in on the person who really needs the product or service.

6
IT'S THE REAL THING
Advertising

Business Rules of Thumb
HALL OF FAME

DAVID OGILVY—In his *Confessions of an Advertising Man*, published in 1963, Mr. Ogilvy detailed the origins of Ogilvy and Mather, an advertising firm which he cofounded. Since that time, the firm has become one of the four biggest advertising agencies in the world, with 140 offices in forty countries. *Time* magazine has called Mr. Ogilvy "the most sought-after wizard in the advertising business."

W. E. PHILLIPS
Chairman and CEO
The Ogilvy Group

In advertising, the more you tell, the more you sell. People will read long advertising copy if it is informative, well presented, and of interest.

BOBBY COHEN
President
Bobby's Weekend Rentals

Be cautious of advertising for ego. Many new or quickly growing companies advertise to spread the name and gain exposure without analyzing whether it will promote sales.

STARCH RESEARCH

NINE ADVERTISING RULES DISCOVERED THROUGH RESEARCH

A two-page spread attracts about 25 percent more readership than a one-page ad.

A half-page ad is about two-thirds as effective as a full page.

A full-page color ad attracts about 40 percent more readers than a black and white one.

Multipage ads attract more readers than single pages or spreads, but not in direct proportion to the number of pages involved.

Position in the front or back of the magazine (outside of the covers) does not matter.

Readership does not drop off when an ad is rerun several times in a magazine.

Photographs are more effective than drawings.

Illustrations showing the product in use are better than static product illustrations.

Ads with people in them score higher.

Black and white ads are about 20 percent more effective than ads with black and one color.

BOARDROOM REPORTS

Find the product's biggest benefit and build the ad copy's headline around it. Then repeat it at least twice: once in the body text, again at the end.

DAVID OGILVY
Founder
Ogilvy & Mather International

When writing an ad, use sentences of no more than twelve words.

JAY CONRAD LEVINSON
Author
Guerrilla Marketing

Your family, friends, and work associates will get tired of an advertisement much more quickly than will the average consumer.

JIM LAMARCA
President
LaMarca Group

Do not allocate a product's ad budget to national media when the product's sales are geographically more limited.

DAVID OGILVY

A good ad will have at least fourteen references to people for every one hundred words of copy.

LYNN PHILLIPS
Professor
Stanford Business School

If using humor in advertising, focus the humor on a salient aspect of the product, don't focus the humor on the user.

McGRAW-HILL LABORATORY OF ADVERTISING
PERFORMANCE

The average cost per reader of ads in business publications is eighteen cents.

MARK RANDALL
Sports Consultant

Heavy advertising won't help an entertainment event which has poor early ticket sales.

DAVID OGILVY

In creating an ad, do research with consumers to determine what promise would be most likely to make them buy your brand.

BRANDON TARTIKOFF
Vice-president, Programming
NBC

TV RULES OF THUMB

Never schedule a show just because you like it.

View skeptically any show whose concept takes longer than ten seconds to explain.

Protect "quality" shows so long as they show hope of eventually reaching a broad audience.

Put funny people in comedies.

Do not schedule programs about weighty subjects on Fridays and Saturdays.

Remember that people watch shows not networks. There is no such thing as network loyalty.

Pick programs with women in mind.

Never challenge a strong show with one of similar appeal.

Every time you consider scheduling something of questionable moral value, look at yourself in the mirror—literally.

All hits are flukes.

DAVID OGILVY

If you are lucky enough to write a good advertisement, repeat it until it stops selling.

ROBERT AABERG
Entrepreneur

The "golden ratio" for any billboard or sign is 5:8—five units of height for eight units of width.

SETH GODIN

Realize that many employees of ad agencies are frustrated novelists and artists. Don't give them a free hand with your budget. Be cheap. Cheap advertising forces them to be clever.

TESTED COPY
Starch Research

Put a headline next to or below the illustration in print ads. Headlines are frequently put at the top of the page, above the illustration. But a study of 2,500 different ads showed that 10 percent fewer readers looked at the copy when it was isolated from the headline.

WILLIAM VAN PELT
Gallup & Robinson Advertising

Specific industrial ads score greater recall than ads that present a generalized benefit.

WILLIAM BERNBACH
Chairman of the Board
Doyle Dane Bernbach

Make the product the star of the ad.

SETH GODIN

There is no such thing as an ad that gives too hard a sell. Don't soft-sell your product—you probably can't afford it.

ROBERT HISRICH
Sloan Management Review

Comparison advertising hasn't been proven to be any more or less effective than noncomparison advertising.

R. CLIFTON LONG
Communications Manager
Mobil

Humorous industrial ads rarely work.

DAVID OGILVY

Unless your advertising contains a BIG IDEA, it will pass like a ship in the night. To recognize a BIG IDEA:

1. Did it make me gasp when I first saw it?
2. Do I wish I had thought of it myself?
3. Is it unique?
4. Does it fit the strategy to perfection?
5. Could it be used for thirty years?

(BIG IDEAS include the Marlboro Man, the Merrill Lynch Bull, and American Express' "Do You Know Me?")

MESSNER, FREDERICK, POPPE & TYSON
Advertising

"How To" headlines are very effective for industrial ads in a business publication.

DAVID OGILVY

Research shows that commercials with celebrities are below average in persuading people to buy products.

MAIL ORDER CONNECTION

Small ads work best when enclosed in borders to keep the eye focused.

LIZ ROBERTS
Cartoonist

For maximum effect when using cartoon characters in your ad, make sure at least 60 percent of the characters are male.

JIM KOBS
Kobs & Brady Advertising

The first right-hand page and the back cover are usually the best places for advertisements. These are followed by the other cover positions and the front section of the magazine.

JAY CONRAD LEVINSON

Repetition is the key to good advertising. For every three advertisements viewed, the average consumer will ignore two. It takes the average consumer nine exposures to an ad before the ad is readily remembered. Thus, a specific ad should be run at least twenty-seven times in media directed toward a specific consumer niche before the ad is changed.

BOARDROOM REPORTS

Save up to 75 percent by buying remnant ad space—that's unsold space the magazine must fill as an issue's deadline approaches.

ADWEEK

Four out of five broadcast commercials use music.

DAVID OGILVY

A successful magazine advertisement should be one-third headline, one-third photo or illustration, and one-third text.

DAVID OGILVY

Black type on a white background is better read than white type reversed on a black background.

" "

7
I'M GLAD YOU ASKED ME THAT
PR and Promotions

GEORGE GLAZER
Senior Vice-president
Hill & Knowlton, Inc.

In a taped TV interview, take all the time you want before answering—they'll edit out the silence. Don't try to stall with a statement such as: "Well, that's a very good question." It sounds evasive.

BUSINESS WEEK

Do anything but the normal office routine—nap, jog, get a facial massage—on the day of a TV interview.

ANA and JOHN KADON
Authors
Successful Public Relations Techniques

A corporation should not present favorable news items on late Friday afternoons or early Saturday.

BERT DECKER
President
Decker Communications

The actual presentation of a speech will likely run one-third longer than it did in practice.

LEE IACOCCA
Chairman of the Board
Chrysler Corporation

In public speaking, start by telling them what you're going to tell them. Then tell them. Finally, tell them what you've already told them.

ANA and JOHN KADON

Use black-and-white photos with newspaper press releases.

DAVID DATABASE

The average company pays about .5 percent of its sales dollar for consumer service.

KIRK HANSON
Professor
Stanford Business School

Always have a PR person present when an executive is interviewed. This will help direct the interview, as well as reducing misquotes.

KIRK HANSON

Always film everything that is filmed by the media.

NATIONAL THRIFT NEWS

When handling the media in a crisis, designate a group of high-level executives as spokespeople. Give their names and business phone numbers to the media.

KIRK HANSON

You can't win when testifying before a congressional committee—you can only hold your own.

A. W. CLAUSEN
President
The World Bank

Every top executive should serve a stint in Washington, D.C.

REGIS MCKENNA
Founder
Regis McKenna Public Relations

Answer the question you want to answer.

── **Business Rules of Thumb** ──
── **HALL OF FAME** ──

REGIS MCKENNA—Mr. McKenna is chairman of Regis McKenna, Inc., an international marketing consulting firm specializing in providing services to leading high-technology companies. He is the author of *The Regis Touch* and is president of the National Commission on Industrial Innovation.

REGIS McKENNA

Don't assume that your listener always makes obvious connections which are crucial to the logic of your message.

REGIS McKENNA

Don't give stories away before their time.

ANA and JOHN KADON

Schedule press conferences for 9:00 A.M.

ROBERT TOWNSEND
Former President, Avis Rent-A-Car
Author, Up the Organization

Customers feel better when their complaints are handled by someone who appears to have a high standing in the organization.

REGIS McKENNA

Some members of the press like to get very friendly and conversational so that you will tell them proprietary information without thinking. Don't let your guard down too much.

REGIS McKENNA

The most effective interview is one where you are relating to your interviewer's interests.

ANA and JOHN KADON

Never speak more than thirty minutes. Impromptu speeches should never be more than five to ten minutes.

ARJAY MILLER
Former President
Ford Motor Co.

Don't do anything you would not be willing to explain on TV.

REGIS McKENNA

If you want something to be off the record, get an agreement before you start talking.

REGIS McKENNA

Look for opportunities to reinforce your key message.

REGIS McKENNA

Keep in control of the conversation.

KIRK HANSON

In dealing with community groups, you must allow the groups to have a pound of flesh in the first meeting (let them shit all over you). Once they have voiced their anger they'll be more trusting.

KIRK HANSON

Any corporate contact with Congress ought to be handled by a constituent of the district rather than a Washington, D.C., employee.

JOHN HANLEY
Chairman of the Board
Monsanto

Work hard, keep your nose clean, and don't talk to the press.

KIRK HANSON

Self-disclosure is better than media disclosure.

KIRK HANSON

All inquiries by the press should be handled by media relations staff.

8
THE ULTIMATE LEMONADE STAND
Retailing

CHARLES REED
Accountant

In the bar or restaurant business, take inventory weekly. More shortages will occur in inventory than in cash receipts.

JEFF MELENDY
Managing Partner
Bull's Texas Cafe

In a restaurant, food is marked up three times direct cost, beer four times, and liquor six times.

CONVENIENCE STORE NEWS INDUSTRY REPORTS

Small retailers in the West tend to use cable and TV advertising almost twice as much as small retailers in the Northeast.

JACK HENRY
President
Security Training Corp.

Internal theft causes greater inventory losses than shoplifting.

LILY WELLS
Clothing Consultant

A 10 percent increase in the price of a standard piece of merchandise in a store will reduce the purchases of that item by 10 percent. A 25 percent increase in the price of a unique piece of merchandise will reduce the purchases by only 10 percent.

SALLY LEDGWICK
Retail Consultant

Twenty-five percent of a retail store's sales typically occur between Thanksgiving and New Year's.

T. JOHN PHILLIPS
Business Consultant

Low-rent locations require more advertising. High-rent locations require less. For all locations, rent and advertising expenses combined should equal 10 percent of sales.

JAY CONRAD LEVINSON
Author
Guerrilla Marketing

The most important factor which causes a consumer to patronize a local retail business is confidence in that business. And confidence is built by advertising.

CHARLES SWAYNE
Owner
Valley View Racquet Club

In health clubs, there are only three times you should increase prices: a) when you announce a major improvement, b) when the major improvement is complete, and c) during your peak season of activity when no one wants to quit. In any case, you can increase your prices each year by as much as 10 percent without worrying about member backlash.

JEFF FURMAN
Business Consultant

The third restaurant to go into a space is generally the one that succeeds.

SYLVIA WEBER
Restaurant Entrepreneur

It takes seven restaurant franchise units to produce the same income as one company-owned restaurant.

BENNY SCHWARTZ
Venture Capitalist

A restaurant's annual revenues should be equal to at least 150 percent of the capital investment cost to build and stock the restaurant (in today's constant dollars).

TOM PETERS
Coauthor
In Search of Excellence

Perception is all there is. If the customer thinks he's right, he's right.

SHARON BLACK
Shoe Retailer

In searching for new store locations, choose a neighborhood in which at least one-third of the stores have been there for over five years and one third of the stores have been there for less than two years.

DEBRA REEVES
Business Statistician

Three times out of four when you see a "closed for remodeling" sign on a retail business, they'll never open again.

PERRY ELLIS
Fashion Designer

If you've got a unique retail product, initially price it high and emphasize its value. Gradually increase the affordability once the product has received some significant attention.

RICHARD M. WHITE
Author
The Entrepreneur's Manual

The average retailer would like to see stock movements of fifty-two times per year.

TED ROLLINS
Car Dealer

Car dealers and antique shops benefit from locations near their competitors. Most other businesses do not.

WHIRLPOOL CORP.

According to consumers, courtesy is the most important quality for a sales clerk.

SYLVIA PORTER
Noted Consumer Advocate

In a retail business, during the first month, the sales volume should increase each day. By the third month, revenues should almost cover operating expenses during the best weeks. By the sixth month, revenues should consistently cover expenses.

CHARLES SWAYNE

A health club should expect a 25 percent turnover in members annually.

Business Rules of Thumb
HALL OF FAME

SYLVIA PORTER—A noted journalist on household and business economics, Ms. Porter's *The Money Book* is a classic source for personal money management. Ms. Porter is world-renowned for making money matters accessible and understandable to the general public.

PROGRESSIVE GROCER'S MARKETING GUIDEBOOK

The average supermarket has six payrolled employees per checkout stand.

KATHY MILLER
President
Activities, Inc.

Put all of the two-seat tables (for couples) near the view windows of your restaurant; these couples will appreciate either the romantic views or the opportunity to ignore each other.

JAY CONRAD LEVINSON

If you're in retail, spend at least 10 percent of your gross sales revenue on advertising, or at least be more aggressive than your competition.

JAN YOUNG
Computer Retailer

Many computer retail stores sell products off-site or by mail. A computer retailer's rent should correspond with the importance of the retail site. For example, if 50 percent of the retailer's sales are to occur at the site, the rent should be 50 percent of that of a competitor that derives all sales on-site.

CYRIL MAGNIN
Former Chairman of the Board
I. Magnin

If you're over forty years old—mentally—you don't belong in retailing.

CHIP CONLEY

The margin on a given retail item in a store is inversely proportional to the number of stores carrying the item.

9
CLIMBING THE CORPORATE LADDER
Organizational Structure

LEONARD PACE
Management Consultant
Deloitte, Haskins & Sells

As the economy weakens, to keep talented people on staff, reassign them to longer-term projects, such as new-product development.

TOM PETERS and BOB WATERMAN
Authors
In Search of Excellence

The task force–reporting level and the seniority of its members should be proportional to the importance of the problem.

SUCCESS MAGAZINE

DELEGATION RULES

1. Controls should be built into a delegated task, right from the beginning.
2. Provide as much information (not how-to) about the task as possible.
3. The method to achieve the results is not as important as the results. ("Do it my way" will choke off the initiative that is needed in successful delegation.)
4. Crucial decisions regarding a delegated task should not be considered the province of the delegator.
5. Be careful in glamorizing a delegated task that may be perceived as pure drudgery.
6. Delegation is not assigning work. It is handing over responsibility for results, along with the authority and decision-making power to achieve results—it is not just giving orders.
7. Learn to trust. It is the bedrock of delegating.
8. Give up some territory. Possession of territory represents power and security.

LESTER KORN
President
Korn-Ferry International

SEVEN TIPS FOR STREAMLINING THE BOARD

1. Shorten Board meetings.
2. Structure the agenda so that serious and urgent issues are given the most attention. Limit the number of topics.
3. Use committees more effectively.

4. Prepare concise reports for Board members before meetings.
5. Provide directors with staff support.
6. Reduce the number of full Board meetings.
7. Compensate directors in line with what a director earns for the same amount of time and responsibility in his or her primary job.

MCKINSEY & CO.

KEY ELEMENTS FOR A TASK FORCE SUCCESS

1. Small number of members
2. Volunteers
3. No paper
4. Encouragement by top management
5. Feedback on the accomplishments of the task force

TOM PETERS and BOB WATERMAN

One dimension—e.g., product or geography or function—should have crystal-clear primacy in the organizational structure.

JOHN NEWSTROM
Associate Professor
University of Minnesota

Training sessions should be kept well under one hour.

SMC HENDRICK, INC.
Management Consultants

Most managers can effectively handle eight or nine subordinates.

THOMAS WHISLER
University of Chicago

DO'S AND DON'TS FOR BOARD MEMBERS

1. Don't set strategy.
2. Don't fight with others on the board—it can shake shareholder confidence.
3. Do your homework.
4. Do participate.
5. Do support the CEO.
6. Do keep your distance from subordinate employees.
7. Don't discuss company business with others.

BEN BAKER
Management Consultant

As a company doubles its staff, it triples its salary and overhead expense.

HENRY VOSS
Entrepreneur

Beware of left-handed managers; they tend to make better creators than managers.

TOM PETERS and BOB WATERMAN

Seek out a high volume of opportunities for good news swapping among salespeople and employees of the company.

PETER DRUCKER
Noted Business Commentator and Author

Any job that has defeated two or three men in succession, even though each performed well in his previous assignments, should be deemed unfit for human beings and must be redesigned.

MYRON BIGGAR
Management Consultant

Have the credit manager report to the chief operating officer, not to the controller, to draw him into the management process.

LEE IACOCCA
Chairman of the Board
Chrysler Corporation

A manager's performance should be reviewed quarterly and he or she should be responsible for establishing new goals, in writing.

JERRY FAVRETTO
Writer

Never ask one of your staff to do something that's normally assigned to another. Even if the other one died.

JAMES GIARDINA
Arthur Young & Co.

Get away from job descriptions for employees and instead define the desired end result. Job descriptions should concern output rather than activities. If you cannot describe some tangible output, the job should not exist.

HARRY COHEN
Partner
Seidman & Seidman, CPAs

Warning signs which indicate a company is outgrowing its organizational structure:

- The owner being unable or unwilling to delegate authority to managers
- Delays in the owner getting answers to important questions
- The owner attending too many meetings

TIMOTHY BRONELLI
Building Contractor

An executive with an office size larger than 200 square feet is likely to be on his way up or on his way out—they don't stabilize at that level.

TIMOTHY BRONELLI

An executive needs a minimum office size of 125 square feet. An additional 2 square feet should be added to the office for each hour the executive works in that office per week. And then double it if the executive is a partner or chief officer of the company.

JODY LESTER
Traveling Salesman

Don't let your accounting staff have any windows. Give the windows to your marketing and promotions staff who can afford to "space out."

SYLVIA STEINBERG
Health Industry Consultants, Inc.

A company with five to ten employees is twice as likely to have a health plus benefit plan as a company with fewer than five employees. And companies with more than ten employees are twice as likely as the companies with five to ten employees.

EUGENE WEBB
Associate Dean
Stanford Business School

The individual with responsibility for implementing a decision should be a part of the decision-making process.

BOARDROOM REPORTS

Give a name to all major company projects. It gives everyone an easy way to refer to a common set of goals.

Business Rules of Thumb
HALL OF FAME

BOARDROOM REPORTS—This is the superior bi-weekly business periodical which provides brief and insightful advice and ideas on a wide-ranging array of business-oriented issues. From the authors' perspective, this periodical has no equal in terms of highlighting successful hints and tips used by business people all over the world.

JERRY FAVRETTO

Give everyone a title. Nothing pleases mankind as much and costs as little. Give everyone their own coffee cup.

INTERNATIONAL MANAGEMENT

Assign people expected to produce creative work to easygoing supervisors.

HARRY COHEN

Any small company with more than six people reporting directly to the president needs to spread the management reporting responsibilities immediately.

BOARDROOM REPORTS

Most workers prefer temporary relocation to being laid off. So, temporarily transfer some key workers to company branches in areas less affected by recessions.

RICHARD M. WHITE
Author
The Entrepreneur's Manual

First-rate men hire first-rate men . . . second-rate men hire third-rate men . . . these third-rate men will then employ the bulk of your company's employees and they tend to select fourth-rate people.

ROBERT SCHAFFER
Consultant

In launching performance-improvement programs, focus immediately on tangible results rather than programs, preparations, and problem solving.

B. F. SKINNER
Noted Psychologist

ON MOTIVATING EMPLOYEES

- Reinforcement ought to be specific, incorporating as much information content as possible.
- Reinforcement should have immediacy.
- Reinforcement should be unpredictable and intermittent.

DR. GERALD OLIVERO
Vice-president
PA International

Favor impulse types for first-line managers.

DR. GERALD OLIVERO

Lean toward people-oriented managers to keep an already well-run operation in tune.

DR. GERALD OLIVERO

Look for sociable and persuasive managers for personnel and public or customer relations.

KARL GRUEN
Union Carbide

An office dimension of 13.5 by 13.5 feet is the optimal office size for a white-collar employee.

ROBERT HENCAULT
Vice-president
Stelco, Inc.

Paying average performers the same as high performers is the most effective demotivator of high performers.

DR. DANIEL LANCER
General Motors

Roughly 70 percent of all chronic absence is alcohol- or drug-related.

MARY KAY ASH
Founder
Mary Kay Cosmetics

Never say, "That's against company policy," unless you have a good explanation to back up the policy.

ROBERT TOWNSEND
Former President, Avis Rent-A-Car
Author, Up the Organization

In delegating responsibility, make the delegates set terms, timetables, and objectives. This procedure makes it possible to measure how they are handling their new responsibilities.

ROBERT SCOTT, JR.
CPA
The Journal of Accountancy

Review bonus plans every two to three years.

McIVOR and BELLE
Authors
The Official Rules

The ratio of time involved in work to time available to work is usually .6 (4.8 hours of an 8-hour day are spent in actual work).

ILLINOIS INSTITUTE OF TECHNOLOGY

It takes about three overtime hours to produce two standard hours' worth of work. For heavy work, count on two hours' time for each hour's worth of output.

HAROLD GENEEN
Former Chairman of the Board
ITT Corp.

Require that all employees bluntly state at the beginning of all memos a summary of the unshakable facts.

BOOZ ALLEN HAMILTON
Management Consultants

Waiting for work takes up to 15 percent of the workday of company clerical employees.

JOAN THALL
Labor Negotiations Consultant

Understand a union's priorities:

1. Union survival
2. Union growth
3. Union profits

4. Union power
5. The benefits the union's members receive
6. Union image
7. The health of your company
8. A combination of minor priorities such as the effects of your labor contract on your company's customers, its effects on the economy

PRODUCTION AND INVENTORY MANAGEMENT REVIEW

Every hour of absenteeism costs the employer 75 percent of the absentee's wage in lost profits.

ZOLTAN MERSZEI
President
Occidental Petroleum

TEN COMMANDMENTS FOR BUSINESS

1. Always have too few people.
2. Judge people carefully. If you do it well, everything will become easier.
3. Seek change, don't just accept it.
4. Center decision making where the action is.
5. Organization follows ability, not the reverse.
6. Fit the organization to the people, not people to the organization.
7. Learn from the past, but invest in the future.
8. Don't just accept responsibility—usurp it.
9. Don't hope for excellence. Demand it, of yourself and others.
10. Develop a vision of what's to come in the world. That is the ultimate insurance of success.

10
THE REVOLVING DOOR
Hiring, Firing, and Career Choices

ROBERT HALF
President
Robert Half International

BEST QUESTIONS FOR A JOB INTERVIEW

- What did you do the day before yesterday—in detail?
- Why do you think we should hire you?
- What are the most difficult aspects of your current job, and how do you approach them?
- Where do you think the power comes from in your organization?
- Tell me three characteristics about yourself.
- What do you think might differentiate you from other applicants?

SETH GODIN

Ask a prospective employee what games he or she likes to play. Most people fall in the Scrabble/Trivial Pursuit category. They tend to be less creative than those employees that play a wide variety of games.

DEBORAH FROEB
Vice-president, Special Assets
First Interstate Bank of Denver

Upon firing a general manager, give the person a precisely defined schedule for when they should vacate the offices. Never allow the person's presence to linger, as this will stagnate the anticipated management transition.

CPA CLIENT BULLETIN

The four most popular executives perks are (in descending order):

1. Physical exams
2. Company cars
3. Club memberships
4. Financial counseling

ROBERT HALF

KEYS TO SUCCESSFUL HIRING

- Focus on accomplishments
- Don't try to force a fit.
- Picture the candidate in the job.
- Give special consideration to motivation.
- Limit the number of decision makers in the process.
- Don't settle—seek the best.
- If you make a mistake, rectify it quickly.

GEORGE MAZZEI
Author
Moving Up

When moving out of a company, recommend someone to replace you, from your staff if possible. This is a courtesy, but also an affirmation that you have done an admirable job of hiring and training.

ROBERT HALF

The best person you interview isn't neccessarily the best person for the job.

ACCOUNTEMPS

Friday afternoon is the time when top managers and personnel executives are most likely to give permanent employees the ax.

BOARDROOM REPORTS

Have all workers sign an agreement to repay any corporate moving allowance if the worker quits in less than six months.

DAVID KANDELA
International Marketing Executive

The end-of-year bonus for an executive of a large corporation should equal one week's salary.

EUGENE WEBB
Associate Dean
Stanford Business School

Never hire a salesman you'd want your daughter to marry.

DON TICHNOR
Farmer

To estimate a yearly salary from an hourly wage, double the wage and change the decimal point to a comma. Thus, $30 per hour becomes $60,000 a year.

MICHAEL FRISCH
Author
Hire the Best: A Practical Guide to Effective Interviewing

The job applicant should be talking about 70 to 80 percent of the time in an interview.

HARRIS HEERY & ASSOCIATES
Adweek

One in five MBAs starting at an average major packaged-goods company will make it to group product manager.

MANAGEMENT PSYCHOLOGY

The average fifty-four-year-old male has had 9.7 employers.

MARK McCORMACK
Author
What They Don't Teach You at Harvard Business School

Beware of the following phrases if they are directed to you:

- **A.** "It may seem like a lateral move, but . . ."
- **B.** "We've created this new position especially for you."
- **C.** "This job really requires the special talent of someone like you."

KAREN O'NEILL
Career Consultant

After thirty, a highly qualified professional should expect to earn his or her age times $1,000 in salary.

C. NORTHCOTE PARKINSON
Noted Business Commentator

The best method to get a top executive to retire early is to give him a superficial promotion so that he is going to lots of conferences. Make sure to send him to conferences which are held at places the maximum distance apart, and in climates offering the sharpest contrast in heat and cold. Not only does this travel prove to be a retirement-accelerator, but it also decreases the executive's influence in the organization, since he is rarely at the home office.

PAUL HELLMAN
Savvy Magazine

Don't accept a job offer without sleeping on it.

RICHARD K. CONNAROE
Editor
Executive Search

In negotiating with an executive you want to hire, expect to offer at least a 20 percent increase over your candidate's present salary, all other issues assumed to be equal.

ROBERT HALF

Plan on spending one week job hunting for every $2,000 in salary and benefits you received in your last job. If your qualifications are particularly high, deduct 20 percent from your search time; if they are low, add 50 percent. If you want to keep your hunt a secret, multiply your final time by two.

ALFRED SLOAN, JR.
Former Chairman of the Board
General Motors

Never make a personnel judgment the first time it comes up. Never fire someone without sleeping on it.

ROBERT HALF

A bad reference is as hard to find as a good employee.

SYLVIA PORTER
Noted Consumer Advocate

For every dollar you earn in wages you ought to be receiving thirty cents in fringe benefits. In recent years, fringe benefits have been increasing at two to three times the rate of increase in cash wages and salaries, or about 10 to 12 percent a year.

ROMAN WEIL
Accounting Professor
University of Chicago Business School

Don't hire an accountant if you need creativity.

THE LEVINSON LETTER

Give exit interviews to popular employees who leave the firm, as it is likely the employee will be quite candid.

SYLVIA PORTER

Don't answer in your own name any "blind" ad (one giving only a box number and not identifying a company). Instead, have a friend cover for you by signing a third-person letter describing your qualifications to help you remain anonymous.

ROBERTA REYNES
Savvy Magazine

The more marketing-oriented a firm is, the more flexible they are in negotiating a salary.

ROBERT HALF

If you think an interview question is discriminatory, it probably is.

RALPH FLETCHER
Venture Magazine

After interviewing a job candidate, make a hypothetical list of the candidate's strengths and weaknesses from your observations. That way, you'll be sure to check with references any potential problems you think need exploring.

ROBERT HALF

FIRING PEOPLE

- Do it in person.
- Don't drag it out.
- Be supertactful.
- Have separation materials at hand.
- Move the person out fast.
- Watch your comments to other employees.
- Analyze what went wrong.

PAUL HELLMAN

To maximize the size of your next job's salary:

1. Let them make the first bid.
2. Ask for 20 percent more than their offer.

CHARLES O'REILLY
University of California at Berkeley

Over one-third of MBA graduates leave their first job in less than two years.

FRANK NEMEYER
Publisher

A company with fewer than one hundred employees may have trouble keeping a personnel manager busy.

MARK McCORMACK

If you are offered any job you want with a new company and you don't know the company that well, ask to head the international division. All else being equal, this is where you can make the most impact in the least amount of time.

HARRIS HEERY ASSOCIATES
Adweek

MANAGEMENT MILESTONES

Marketing Assistant: age 24
Assistant Product Manager: 26
Product Manager: 28
Senior Product Manager: 30
Group Product Manager: 33
VP/Marketing: 39
General Management: 43

HENRY RIGGS
Vice-president
Stanford University

The most useful first experiences for the aspiring young general manager are (a) selling and (b) managing a group comprised of individuals from substantially different socioeconomic backgrounds.

EUGENE WEBB

California-based firms should recruit out-of-state executives during the winter.

DONALD L. HUGHES
President
Hurricane Shutter Co.

Get a letter of resignation from any employee who is leaving voluntarily. This documents the reason for leaving in case an unemployment claim is filed later on.

DAVID STUCKY
Sales Representative
IBM

"Career" is a dirty word, as it connotes that you will have a series of jobs with some linear progression.

CHERYL RUSSELL
Demographer

During a job interview, never spend more than sixty seconds answering a question.

ANONYMOUS PROFESSOR
Stanford Business School

MBA's from top schools earn about $1,000 annually for every hour they are expected to work in the average week.

11
FIRST IMPRESSIONS
Interpersonal Relations

DALE CARNEGIE
Noted Author and Philosopher

Rather than telling an associate, "You look good in that suit," tell the person, "That suit looks good on you."

SETH GODIN

Secretaries are people too. Treating them as such will dramatically increase job satisfaction and productivity.

KENNETH BLANCHARD and **SPENCER JOHNSON**
Authors
The One Minute Manager

THE ONE-MINUTE REPRIMAND

1. Tell people *beforehand* that you are going to let them know how they are doing in no uncertain terms.
2. Reprimand people immediately.
3. Tell people what they did wrong—be specific.
4. Tell people how you feel about what they did wrong—and in no uncertain terms.

5. Stop for a few seconds of uncomfortable silence to let them *feel* how you feel.
6. Shake hands, or touch them in a way that lets them know you are honestly on their side.
7. Remind them how much you value them.
8. Reaffirm that you think well of them but not of their performance in this situation.
9. Realize that when the reprimand is over, it's over.

HAROLD LEAVITT
Professor
Stanford Business School

Don't take the early task decisions made by a group too seriously. Groups tend to rush into decisions, often poorly thought-out ones.

BOARDROOM REPORTS

Use the word "leadership" rather than "power." People are intimidated by the word "power."

ERIC FERMOND
French Military Officer

When introducing yourself to someone for the first time, enunciate your name very precisely—they will more likely remember the name if you stress the enunciation.

DALE CARNEGIE

You should be suspicious of someone who nods and speaks in the affirmative, but has their arms crossed.

DALE CARNEGIE

TEN WAYS TO BE A LEADER

Begin with praise and honest appreciation.

Call attention to people's mistakes indirectly.

Talk about your own mistakes before criticizing the other person.

Ask questions instead of giving direct orders.

Let the other person save face.

Praise the slightest improvement and praise every improvement. Be "hearty in your approbation and lavish in your praise."

Give the other person a fine reputation to live up to.

Use encouragement. Make the fault easy to correct.

Make the other person happy about doing the thing you suggest.

MARQ VON RADDEN
German Fashion Designer

If you have to tell a co-worker or client bad news, make sure you call them before they call you—you should be the one to alert them.

ELAINE YARBROUGH
Management Consultant

Never touch the person whom you are criticizing, as this is like rubbing it in.

STANLEY JONES
Professor
University of Colorado

Don't touch the person you're talking to if it interrupts a task or conversation.

JAMES VAN LARE
President
Training by Design

TIPS FOR GIVING NEGATIVE FEEDBACK

A. Use "I" in observations instead of "you."
B. Be specific in criticisms.
C. Make feedback timely.
D. Keep it brief.
E. Focus on the effect of behavior.
F. Criticize only what it's possible to change.

HOCK HOPKINS
Restaurateur

When a person prefaces a statement with "In all honesty" or "To tell you the truth" or "To be perfectly candid with you," realize that the person is not being perfectly candid with you.

DALE CARNEGIE

If you're wrong, admit it quickly and emphatically.

D. KLEIN
Painter

When uncertain of a person's sincerity, watch their shoulders. You should doubt anyone who is speaking with strong emotion and relaxed shoulders.

BOARDROOM REPORTS

Best time to criticize a subordinate is early in the day. The worker has time to think it over and to discuss it later if necessary.

N. BRUCE ASHWILL
President
Bishop-Hawk, Inc.

Never ask a question you don't want to hear the answer to.

MARY KAY ASH
Founder
Mary Kay Cosmetics

Sandwich every bit of criticism between two heavy layers of praise.

DAVID OGILVY
Founder
Ogilvy & Mather International

Do not summon people to your office—it frightens them. Instead, go to see them in their offices. This makes you visible throughout the firm.

HAROLD LEAVITT

Don't cut off the early chatter and small talk of a new group —the tendency of people to tell stories that seem irrelevant is part of the process of group integration. Don't interrupt them as irrelevancies which must be suppressed.

N. BRUCE ASHWILL

If you're interested in obtaining something from someone else, always preface your request with "I have a favor to ask you," as people hate turning down favors.

12
LET'S DO LUNCH
Business Life, Dressing, Eating, and Success

BILL KAHANE
Vice-president
Morgan Stanley

Shine your shoes at least once a week.

ROGER RUSSELL
Writer

For maximum self-promotion as a new employee in a midwestern or southern company, become the committee head of the annual company picnic.

JOHN T. MOLLOY
Author
Dress for Success

10 RULES FOR MEN WHO WANT TO DRESS LIKE AN EXECUTIVE

   1. Beige raincoats, not dark ones.
   2. Don't take off your suit jacket unless you have to.

3. Brown shoes with brown suits, black shoes with everything else.
4. Socks that reach over the calf.
5. Silk tie—dark blue with small white dots (no bow ties).
6. Long wallet that fits into the inside suit pocket.
7. Dark cordovan, not black, attaché case.
8. Black umbrella; not a fold-up model.
9. Never wear a short sleeve shirt or a shiny shirt.
10. Never wear green.

ROGER RUSSELL
Writer

For maximum self-promotion as a new employee in a northeastern company, join the best business social club and take your superiors to wine and dine there.

ROBERT RINGER
Winning Through Intimidation

A visiting businessman is perceived with greater respect than an in-town businessman. When possible, emphasize that you are from out-of-town, as people will listen to what you have to say more carefully.

ROGER RUSSELL

For maximum self-protection as a new employee in a western company, become director of the company's sports fitness program.

CRAIG SLATON
Political Lobbyist

At business lunches, always name your desired brand of alcohol when ordering a mixed drink (e.g., Tanqueray and tonic). It demonstrates strength and decisiveness to your associates.

CHIP CONLEY

The best time to meet with a potential heavyweight investor is Sunday brunch. It's more likely that you will get quality time with this person and the investor will be less preoccupied.

PAVLOO LOUPAKIS
Greek Shipping Magnate

Never pick up the check if your lunch date outranks you.

GRANT McLAREN
Entrepreneur

Exercising during the lunch hour makes your afternoon twice as productive.

HOWARD FLINKER
Analyst
Reich & Tang, Inc.

Never use a business lunch to accomplish the kind of business that can more efficiently be done in an office.

KEN JACOBS
Associate
Goldman, Sachs

Four out of five times, "pressing business" will threaten your treasured vacation. Call in sick the day before you are scheduled to take off for a vacation so that you are not susceptible to being asked to cancel the vacation because an urgent assignment is handed to you at the last minute.

MARK McCORMACK
Author
What They Don't Teach You at Harvard Business School

Never make restaurant reservations for fewer than three (particularly in New York, Paris, and London), as you will be stuck in a tiny, uncomfortable table in the corner otherwise.

MARIAN McCONNELL
Corporate Strategist
Turner Broadcasting Co.

Count on New Yorkers taking a two-hour lunch.

SUSAN BIXLER
Author
The Professional Image

Darker business suit colors will be more serviceable when you are mixing and matching.

SUSAN BIXLER

Best basic colors for men in suits, jackets, trousers: medium blue, navy, gray, beige, and camel.

SUSAN BIXLER

Men should not buy black suits, as they are simply too overpowering.

SUSAN BIXLER

Best basic colors for women in suits, blazers, and skirts: black, burgundy, blue, brown, gray, beige, and camel.

RICHARD M. WHITE, JR.
Author
The Entrepreneur's Manual

If you suspect that an evening on the town with a salesman might lead to trouble, invite the man's wife to join you. It's cheaper in the long run.

Business Rules of Thumb
HALL OF FAME

RICHARD M. WHITE, JR.—Mr. White is a well-respected business consultant and author. His book *The Entrepreneur's Manual* is likely the most comprehensive book ever written on business start-ups and spin-offs.

MARK McCORMACK

At a business meal, do not turn to business until the meal has been ordered and the menus taken away.

MIREK SPRINGER
German Actor

When lunching with someone you want to impress, pick the restaurant and make sure you arrive there first.

INC. MAGAZINE

Don't leave the job of arranging airline reservations and hotel accommodations to your secretary. A good travel agent is likely to do the job better.

GRANT McLAREN

An executive's productivity in the afternoon is equal to one over the number of drinks imbibed at lunch. For example, three drinks will cause the executive to be one-third as productive as normal.

E. MELVIN PINSEL and LIGOTA DIENHART
Authors
Power Lunching

Don't order drinks served with a paper umbrella.

C. NORTHCOTE PARKINSON
Noted Business Commentator

At a cocktail party, the guests will naturally filter to the left side of the room as they enter it (the clockwise movement theory), so if you are interested in meeting some new people, place yourself slightly inside the left side of the doorway.

Business Rules of Thumb
HALL OF FAME

C. NORTHCOTE PARKINSON—Best known for his satiric book, *Parkinson's Law*, Mr. Parkinson is a prolific historian who has studied human nature and how it relates to organizational structure. His encyclopedia of laws such as "Work expands so as to fill the time available" and "Delay is the deadliest form of denial" has made him one of the premier philosophers of our time.

SUSAN KROWNBURROW
Interior Designer

When decorating your office, use the combined skills of your executive secretary and your controller. One will control taste while the other will control cost.

13
BUILDING
CHARACTER
Habits, Ethics, and Wisdoms

ROBERT TILLMAN
Director of Marketing
Paradise Systems, Inc.

Never sleep with someone who reports to you.

EXECU-TIME

Make your important phone calls early in the morning.

JERVIS B. WEBB
President and Chairman
Jervis B. Webb Co.

Keep a little book that lists each person and each conversation
you have with them on a daily basis.

MARK McCORMACK
Author
What They Don't Teach You at Harvard Business School

If you are calling for a simple answer to a question, to confirm something, or to get the other party's support or agreement, couch the call in such a way that silence means consent: "Please have Mr. So and So call me only if he disagrees."

NAPOLEON HILL
Author
Think and Grow Rich

NAPOLEON HILL'S MAJOR ATTRIBUTES OF LEADERSHIP

1. Unwavering courage
2. Self-control
3. A keen sense of justice
4. Definiteness of decision
5. Definiteness of plans
6. The habit of doing more than paid for
7. A pleasing personality
8. Sympathy and understanding
9. Mastery of detail
10. Willingness to assume full responsibility
11. Cooperation

┌─ **Business Rules of Thumb** ─┐
└── **HALL OF FAME** ──

NAPOLEON HILL—Mr. Hill conducted one of the most thorough and exhaustive business research projects ever initiated. Over the twenty-year project, he interviewed thousands of successful businessmen and leaders, including Henry Ford, Andrew Carnegie, John D. Rockefeller, Woodrow Wilson, and Theodore Roosevelt. *Think and Grow Rich*, the famous book which documented the findings of the project, is one of the most respected resources on the subject of how to be successful.

HENRY FORD
Founder
Ford Motor Co. (and the inventor of charcoal briquettes)

Reach a decision promptly and decisively and change that decision slowly.

CHIP CONLEY

The ideal time to return phone calls is between 5:00 P.M. and 5:30 P.M., unless you're calling the government or I.B.M.

RICHARD S. SLOMA
Author
No Nonsense Management

Reduce the anxiety in decision making by learning to differentiate between decisions that can be reversed and those that cannot. Move quickly with those capable of being nullified. Go slower on those that are final.

DONALD RUMSFELD
Former Presidential Adviser

Read and listen for what is missing. Many advisers—in and out of government—are quite capable of telling the President how to improve what has been proposed, or what's gone wrong. Few seem capable of sensing what isn't there.

S. T. CONLEY, SR.
President
Bancap Investment Group

Don't promise early . . . always promise late.

STELLA DOCKWORTH
Executive Secretary
Globin Associates, Inc.

An executive should clean the desk tops of his office and rid them of unimportant documents once a week. Files should be weeded monthly.

JOSEPH STEIN
Business Consultant

There are three valid answers to a yes or no question: yes, no, and no decision right now.

Eighty percent of all bad decisions are snap decisions.

Good managers make the best decisions after sleeping on it.

BOARDROOM REPORTS

Require a disposal date on all memos so the recipient doesn't have to take the initiative in deciding how long to keep the memo. This also cuts down on the need for file cabinets.

PAUL FARGIS
Independent Book Producer

The cost of writing, typing, filing, and mailing a single business letter is at least $4.50. If you can make your point quickly, a long-distance phone call is usually cheaper than mail.

EXECU-TIME

Memos should confirm discussions or present new ideas, but they are wasteful as a means of arguing the issues.

SETH GODIN

THE 80/20 RULE

In almost all endeavors, 20 percent of the group produces 80 percent of the results. Concentrating on the 20 percent of the workers, customers, etc., that provide the 80 percent is the most productive way to spend your time.

MARK McCORMACK

Do the things that everyone else has to do at the times when everyone else isn't doing them.

14
THE MORE THE MERRIER?
Effective Meetings

BOARDROOM REPORTS

6 WAYS TO INCREASE MEETING EFFICIENCY

A. Eliminate unimportant meetings.
B. Streamline attendance.
C. Conduct meetings after hours.
D. Lock the door.
E. Make conference rooms uncomfortable.
F. Stick to the agenda.

CHIP CONLEY

Creative meetings which are used for brainstorming should always occur in the same location—a room or other place which is used exclusively for this purpose. This promotes a Pavlovian reaction when those present approach or enter the room.

DR. ERIC M. BEINSTOCK
Managing Director
The Edward deBono School of Thinking

For a successful meeting, a rule that two positive points be presented about an idea before one negative comment is made should be implemented.

J. GEOFFREY RAWLINSON
Author
Creative Thinking and Brainstorming

New-idea meetings need at least five people and preferably twelve—mix ages and backgrounds. At the end, go back to the wildest two ideas and see what innovations they inspire.

PETER F. DRUCKER
Noted Business Commentator and Author

Spending 25 percent of one's time in meetings is the sign of a manager's malorganization.

LORRAINE ARDMORE
Management Consultant

Twelve is the maximum-size group which can be expected to be productive.

LANE KIRKLAND
President
AFL-CIO

The usefulness of any meeting is inversely proportional to the size of the group.

JENNY BRICKLER
Entrepreneur

Bring a kitchen timer with you to all meetings with your
attorney. Let it ding every fifteen minutes to remind you that
time is money.

MARK McCORMACK
Author
What They Don't Teach You at Harvard Business School

The time a meeting is to begin and the time it is to end should
be established as early as possible, committed to paper, and
distributed to every attendee. Meetings that begin at an odd-
ball time—10:15 as opposed to 10:30—are also generally at-
tended with greater punctuality.

PETER F. DRUCKER

At the beginning of a meeting, state the specific purpose of
the meeting and be sure that there is agreement among those
present. At the end of the meeting, relate the conclusions to
the original purpose.

Business Rules of Thumb
HALL OF FAME

PETER F. DRUCKER—With the publication of his first book, *The End of Economic Man*, in 1939, Mr. Drucker established himself as a trenchant, unorthodox, and independent analyst of politics, economics, and society. Today, he is considered the founding father of the discipline of management, and is the most influential and widely read thinker and writer on modern organizations and their management.

RICK RUNDELL
Building Contractor

Schedule creative meetings on Monday and Friday and decision-making meetings on Tuesday through Thursday.

SETH GODIN

There are basically two kinds of meetings: meetings for approval and meetings for idea generation. Be careful not to combine them.

PHILIP LONG
Forest Ranger

No meeting should ever last longer than two hours.

TOM KOHLER
Film Producer

If you see a person cross his arms in a meeting, proceed cautiously and focus on his doubts.

EUGENE WEBB
Associate Dean
Stanford Graduate School of Business

Never leave a meeting without clearly defining what needs to be done next.

GERALD I. NIERENBERG
Author
The Art of Negotiation

In a situation where you want people to look to you as a person of authority, try to sit at the head of the table.

EILEEN SHANAHAN
New York Times

The length of a meeting rises with the square of the number of people present.

RICHARD M. WHITE
Author
The Entrepreneur's Manual

A trick to shorten meetings—remove all the chairs from the conference room, lower the temperature to 62 degrees, and don't allow the air to get stale—you'll discover that stand-up meetings take about half the time as sit-down meetings.

PAUL MILLS and BERNARD ROBERTS
Partners
Mills Roberts Associates

In trying to elicit a response from someone in a meeting, refrain from direct "why" questions ("Why do you feel that way?"), as these can be threatening. Instead, ask, "What are your reasons?"

MARK McCORMACK

In a first meeting with someone who's skeptical of you, do exactly the opposite of what the person expects.

KURT WILSON
Party-Throwing Entrepreneur

Always start a meeting with one member of the group telling about his or her most embarrassing personal experience relating to the subject matter. This tends to lighten up the group and provide for a free flow of information.

JEAN GOUGH
Pastry Chef

Call creative meetings for early in the morning or late in the evening.

WINSTON FLETCHER
Author
Meetings, Meetings

Bad news shouldn't be sugar-coated when delivered in face-to-face meetings.

C. NORTHCOTE PARKINSON
Noted Business Commentator

The amount of time spent on any item of the agenda will be inversely proportional to the sums involved. A committee member will have a vanishing interest when the discussion revolves around larger and larger numbers. The point of vanishing interest represents the sum the individual committee member is willing to lose on a bet or send to a charity.

15
OF SWAMPLAND AND SKYSCRAPERS

Real Estate

MONEY MAGAZINE

A new mortgage must be at least two percentage points lower than the existing one to make up for the up-front fees charged by lenders.

JOHN B. ALLEN
Director of Investment Marketing
Grubb & Ellis Co.

TEN BIGGEST ERRORS MADE BY INVESTORS

1. Buying in poor location
2. Buying an intrinsically poor property
3. Failing to manage the investment properly, especially failure to maximize rents
4. Buying solely for tax benefits
5. Ignoring good marketing practices
6. Concentrating too much on price, and failing to negotiate profitable terms

7. Overleveraging the investment, thus paying too much and creating a possible crisis when it's time to refinance or sell
8. Failure to understand at what point in the income cycle you are buying or selling
9. Failure to look at the possible resale climate, or ignoring holding period determination when you buy
10. Failure to get professional condition reports on the property

TEN TIPS ON MANAGING AT A PROFIT

1. Do a thorough credit check on each tenant.
2. Check rent default history.
3. Collect all rents by cashier's check, money order, or in cash.
4. Rent to tenants with stable employment histories.
5. Maintain a light occupancy load; maximum two tenants per bedroom.
6. Keep common areas well lighted.
7. Minimize landscape upkeep. Install boulders, rocks, gravel, dry landscaping, ivy—not grass.
8. Keep leases month-to-month or quite short (six months).
9. Install laundry and vending machines.
10. Minimize recreation areas.

BRADLEY COLEMAN
Partner
Tefic Brokerage

The complete renovation of an office building takes approximately 50 percent of the time to build a new building.

CHIP CONLEY

When using seller-financing to buy a building in a transition area, require that the financing extend through at least one complete turnover of the leases in order to ratchet up the property's value for future refinancing.

MONEY MAGAZINE

A good adjustable rate mortgage (ARM) ought to have an initial interest rate that is three percentage points below the price of fixed-rate loans.

GRANT LOBDELL
Real Estate Investor

The replacement cost is the most reliable long-term yardstick of building value.

TRAMMELL CROW
Founder
The Trammell-Crow Companies

In a luxury hotel, there should be one thousand square feet of public space per guest room, and one employee on payroll per occupied guest room.

CHIP CONLEY

In a market with stable demand, an increase of 5 percent in the vacancy rate will lead to a 10 percent reduction in rents.

HOW MUCH HOUSE CAN I AFFORD?*

Monthly Income	Annual Percentage Rate										
	8.00%	8.50%	9.00%	9.50%	10.00%	10.50%	11.00%	11.50%	12.00%	12.50%	13.00%
$7,000	$312,000	$301,000	$291,000	$283,000	$272,000	$263,000	$255,000	$247,000	$239,000	$232,000	$225,000
6,000	268,000	259,000	250,000	242,000	234,000	226,000	219,000	212,000	206,000	199,000	193,000
5,000	225,000	217,000	209,000	202,000	196,000	189,000	183,000	177,000	172,000	167,000	162,000
4,000	181,000	175,000	169,000	163,000	157,000	152,000	147,000	143,000	138,000	134,000	130,000
3,000	137,000	132,000	128,000	123,000	119,000	115,000	111,000	108,000	104,000	101,000	98,000
2,000	94,000	90,000	87,000	84,000	81,000	78,000	76,000	73,000	71,000	69,000	66,000

*Assumes you pay ⅓ of take-home pay in housing costs and the bank lends you 80 percent of the value of the house.

KAY WILLIAMS
Money Magazine

In selling your house, avoid any offer that is contingent on the buyer selling his house.

ALAN M. FIELDS
Forbes Magazine

A hotel should make money with 60 to 70 percent occupancy and with room rates that divide construction costs per room by 1000.

CHIP CONLEY

In leasing a new mid-rise or low-rise building which has ground-floor retail space, give first priority to finding a tenant or tenants for that ground floor. Regardless of how much of the office space is occupied, the public will perceive the building as a loser if it is vacant on the ground floor.

KAY WILLIAMS

Put your home on the market in the spring: 71 percent of all home sales occur between April and July.

ROBERT AABERG
Entrepreneur

Mini warehouses (storage facilities) typically are supported by 60 percent residential tenants and 40 percent commercial tenants.

ALEX CRAWFORD
Real Estate Consultant

Real estate cycles tend to last seven years, with year one being the time coming out of a decline, year four being the lowest vacancy, year five being the peak building, and year seven being the trough.

CHIP CONLEY

The cost of shell structural work to a major office renovation project ought to be 20 percent less expensive than that of a new office building, but the cost of interior tenant improvements is likely to be at least 10 percent more expensive because of the renovated structure's idiosyncrasies.

FRANK WHEELER
Real Estate Leasing Agent
Royal LePage

A six-month free rent period at the start of a five-year lease is equal to a 14 percent discount in the present value of the cost of the lease (rather than a 10 percent discount).

FRANK WHEELER

Once a lease has been signed, there's a 90 percent chance the tenant will move in.

CHIP CONLEY

The internal rate of return for a real estate investment should be 6.5 to 7 percent points above the rate of inflation.

ROBERT GORLOW
Real Estate Executive
Prudential Development

Soft costs should equal approximately one-third of hard costs on a typical real estate development project.

MARK CONROE
Vice-president
Mozart Development Co.

A developer can never give too many concessions to a tenant or lease a building too fast. Typically, just the opposite happens and the developer waits too long to give the concessions.

SECURITY MANAGEMENT

For residential apartments, houses, and condominiums, change locks every five years.

SYLVIA PORTER
Noted Consumer Advocate

The proportions of the cost of an average house are: labor, 15 percent; materials, 35 percent; land, 26 percent; builder's overhead and profit, 14 percent; and financing costs, 10 percent.

VINCENT MOONEY
President
Condo Home Realtors

Middle-income condos should sell for 25 percent less than the middle-income homes in the area.

TOM WOLFE
Writer

Rental property should sell for about one hundred times its monthly gross rental income.

JOHN TODD
Landscape Architect

Don't pay more than three times your annual income for a house.

DOUGLAS KESSLER
Pension Fund Real Estate Adviser

The most valuable lot at an intersection is at the southwest corner.

CHIP CONLEY

A Triple-A-rated retail tenant is more valuable than a comparable Triple-A-rated office tenant because the risk of retail failure is higher and the turnover is greater.

E. MANKIN
Journalist

One acre will park a hundred cars.

RANCE O'DAY
Real Estate Broker

Buy the ugliest house in the best neighborhood, never buy the best house in the ugliest neighborhood.

RICHARD TRUBO
Consumer Advocate

Indoor home improvements add more value to a home than do outdoor improvements.

SOL L. RABIN
Director of Investment Research
TCW Realty Advisors

A real estate development project's return on cost is significantly more impacted by lowering the contract rental rate than by increasing the length of time to lease up the project; this suggests that in an overbuilt environment, it is advantageous to wait for the market to tighten up rather than to lease space now at cut-rate rents.

RICHARD TRUBO

The cost of a custom-built home will be at least 20 percent above the purchase price of the exact same home of standard design.

WILLIAM PAYNE
Building Supervisor

A well-planned office building should be able to accommodate one person for every 225 square feet of floor space.

MICHAEL HAMMAN
Building Contractor

The greater the price spread in a given neighborhood, the greater the potential for significantly increasing the value of the less expensive homes.

AL MAHER
Property Management Vice-president
Northwest Asset Management

In hiring for a large commercial real estate development project, never hire your architect, contractor, property manager, and broker without first having them sit down, meet together, and discuss the best strategies for the design, construction, marketing, and management of the property . . . it must be a coordinated team effort.

DOUGLAS KESSLER

Baltimore Rule: The corner lot is worth the sum of the two contiguous lots.

RON KAUFMAN
Veteran Rehab Developer

The first thing you should do in renovating a building is clean and paint the exterior so that people will quickly notice a change.

JOHN B. ALLEN

On average, when an apartment unit turns over, it takes half a month to rerent the unit. And it costs half a month's rent to refurbish the unit. So a 50 percent annual turnover ratio will lead to approximately 4 percent lost income due to turnover.

JAKE O'CONNOR
Apartment Builder

Rents for a one-bedroom apartment in the same building as a studio will be 33 percent higher than the studio. The same ratio exists as you compare two bedrooms to one bedroom and three bedrooms to two bedrooms.

ROBERT AABERG

Office space rents increase in direct proportion with the height of the floor.

CHIP CONLEY

A typical real estate development project budget should allocate 20 percent to land costs, 60 percent to hard construction costs, and 20 percent to soft construction costs (tenant improvements, architect/engineer fees, interest costs).

ALBERT DONNELLY
President
Donnelly Development

In building out an office space to a tenant's requirements (prior to their move-in) a landlord should try not to spend more than 10 percent of the cumulative gross rental income being paid by the tenant over the term of the lease.

MICHAEL FEDERMAN
Vice-president
Federman Construction Consultants

Renovation generally saves 10 to 15 percent of the cost of new construction.

JERRY DAVIS
Author
Rehabbing for Profit

If you're looking to renovate a building, buy on a block where at least a third or more of the buildings show some signs of recent renovation or improvement.

CHIP CONLEY

Maintenance costs for a small to medium-sized apartment building should equal 2.5 percent of gross revenues, while management costs should equal an additional 5 percent.

AXIOM

The three most important considerations in analyzing a property: Location, Location, Location.

ANDREW CARNEGIE
Tycoon

Ninety percent of all millionaires became so through owning real estate.

ROBERT AABERG

On average, a community should have four square feet of mini-warehouse space per capita.

16
BULLS AND BEARS
Stock Market, Investments, and Personal Finance

ROBERT WADSWORTH
President
Robert H. Wadsworth & Associates

In starting a stock market mutual fund, figure on spending $200 to attract each shareholder.

WILLIAM DAVID MONTAPERT
Author
The Omega Strategy

Trade with the trend and don't chase stocks. If the trend is up, buy on dips. If the trend is down, sell on rallies.

KEVIN REYNOLDS
Stock Analyst

Buy stocks whose current price/earnings ratio is 60 percent or less of its historic price-earnings ratio over the previous sixty months.

WILLIAM DAVID MONTAPERT

Purchase stocks that are underowned by the institutions. This means you are more likely to benefit from the institutions' buying power than suffer from their massive selling pressure when and if they change their minds.

EDWARD DYL and STANLEY MARTIN, JR.
Professors
University of Wyoming

Make stock purchases near the close of trading on Mondays and stock sales near the close of trading on Fridays. Studies have shown that stock prices typically drop on Mondays and then progressively rise during the week.

WILLIAM DAVID MONTAPERT

Look for stocks whose future indicated growth rates exceed current price/earnings ratios by a factor of two or more.

B. J. BEAL, JR.
Oil Executive

Buy rumor, sell fact.

BARRY ZISKIN
President
The Opportunity Prospector

In anticipating a bear market, shift all investments into companies with price-earnings ratios of ten or less.

CHIP CONLEY

The results of a stock in any year are inversely proportional to the predictions of the most publicized "stock-pickers."

ELAINE GARZARELLI
Shearson Lehman Brothers
Money Magazine

When the T-bill rate moves 20 percent above its most recent low, watch for a 10 percent to 15 percent correction in stocks.

GRIFFIN DOLE
Stockbroker

When one public company purchases another public company, 75 percent of the time the stock price of the purchasing company will go down while the purchased company will go up.

J. McDONALD WILLIAMS, ESQ.
Managing Partner
Trammell-Crow Companies

Make sure to sell short any industry to which lawyers seem to be flocking.

JEFF DOW
Barret & Worthington

When investing in stamps, buy the best quality you can find.

JOHN CASTELLANOS
Stockbroker

Study the stock purchasing and sales behavior of the executives of the company in which you are considering purchasing (this is available in various periodicals). Buy when they're buying and sell when they're selling.

JONATHON KRASS
Partner
E.F. Hutton

Eighty percent of the individual private investors will lose money in the stock market.

JUSTIN MAMIS and ROBERT MAMIS
Authors
When to Sell

Use stop orders effectively even if the stock rises. Each time the price advances, cancel the old stop order and enter a new one at 10 percent below the current market price.

LOUIS RUKEYSER
Business Journalist

When skirts get higher (as they did, for example, in the 1920s and 1960s), stocks will head in the same direction.

MARTIN E. ZWEIG
Publisher
Zweig Forecast

The stock market tends to discount unfavorable news in advance and to rally in anticipation of, rather than as a result of, favorable news.

MONEY MAGAZINE

When market action is front-page news, the averages continually make new highs, and cocktail-party chatter consists of stock talk, *sell everything!*

PETER DEHASS
Portfolio Strategist
L.F. Rothschild, Unterberg, Towbin

Eighty percent of the issues traded go with the overall market trend.

ROBERT S. SALOMON, JR.
Partner
Salomon Brothers Investment Bank

Look for a growth company that yields 3 percent or more on its current price and pays out no more than 44 percent of its earnings as dividends. If this company continues to grow, it is likely that it will swiftly move up to a 50 percent payout ratio.

THE AMERICAN ASSOCIATION OF INDIVIDUAL INVESTORS

Don't move a substantial portion of your wealth into or out of the market at one time. Ease in, ease out.

RICHARD TRUBO
Consumer Advocate

Life insurance coverage should be four to five times the breadwinner's annual income.

ROBERT A. KENNEDY and TIMOTHY J. WATTS
Authors
Personal Economics: A Guide to Financial Health and Well Being

PERSONAL FINANCIAL RATIOS

- Total Liabilities/Assets: 30% or less
- Liquid Assets/Total Assets: 25% or more
- Savings/Cash Income: 10% or more
- Income Tax/Cash Income: 25% or less

YALE HIRSCH
Publisher
Stock Trader's Almanac

The most powerful single day in the market in recent years is the fifth trading session before year-end.

YALE HIRSCH

October is the best month of the year in which to purchase stocks.

THE AMERICAN ASSOCIATION OF INDIVIDUAL INVESTORS

Don't buy stock that is included in the Fortune 500 or Standard & Poor's 500. The chances of such stocks being undervalued are virtually nil.

STEVEN BACH
World Traveler

Sell short any stock which reaches the cover of a major weekly business periodical.

PETER DEHAAS

Market moves usually exhaust themselves after traveling a maximum of 25 percent up or down from the forty-week moving average of the Dow Jones Industrial Average, S&P's 500 Index, and the NYSE Composite Index.

MONEY MAGAZINE

Bull markets seldom last longer than forty-eight months.

LOUIS RUKEYSER

Look at the restaurant page in the paper and check the ads for Chinese New Year dinners. In years symbolized by bold animals (for example, 1985 was the Year of the Bull), the Dow Jones will leap forward; in years symbolized by weak animals (for example, 1981 was the Year of the Chicken), the Dow Jones will drop.

JOSEPH BARTHEL
Butcher & Singer

If trading exceeds 250 million shares and the Dow seesaws as much as twenty-five points in one day, sell.

LOUIS RUKEYSER

When a team from the old premerger National Football League wins the Super Bowl in January, the stock market will finish higher for the year.

JONATHAN MARCUS
Manager
Deak-Perera

When investing in metals, buy several times a year. Buy more ounces when the price is low, and less when the price is high.

JAMES E. STOWERS
President
Twentieth Century Investors, Inc.

TACTICS FOR A DOWN MARKET

- Shed stocks with flattened earnings.
- Switch to stocks with earnings that have a good chance to rebound sharply.
- Don't get hung up on market timing.

HENRY BLOCK
President
H&R Block

When investing in art, stick to one area, or even one artist.

GERALD LOEB
The Battle for Investment Survival

The greatest safety lies in putting all your eggs in one basket and watching the basket.

CHRISTOPHER H. STINSON
CoEvolution Quarterly Magazine

For small investments, a stock needs to increase 10 percent in value just to break even after the broker's fees.

BOARDROOM REPORTS

The stock market rarely advances more than ten or twelve days in a row without a minor setback. On a longer-term basis, it rarely rises more than six or seven weeks without a setback or "correction" that lasts two to four weeks.

BARRY ZISKIN

In anticipating a bear market, look for companies which have:

- Shown six consecutive years of more than 10 percent growth in pretax operating income
- Shown a 20 percent annual compounded growth rate (exclusive of acquisitions and divestitures)
- Working capital in excess of market valuation

ANNIE O.
Palm Reader

In even years, buy stocks of companies with two syllables or multiples of two in their names. In odd years, buy stocks of companies with an odd number of syllables in their names. In leap years, don't buy stocks.

17
STARS, DOGS, AND CASH COWS
Business Strategy

JOHN HANLEY
President
Monsanto

Set a maximum of three to five corporate goals in a year.

TOM PETERS and BOB WATERMAN
Authors
In Search of Excellence

Objectives should be activities, not abstract financials.

CHIP CONLEY

A new management team for a company will likely have a more immediate impact on net income than gross income.

ROBERT W. JOHNSON
Former Chairman
Johnson & Johnson

Never acquire a business you don't know how to run.

PETER DRUCKER
Noted Business Commentator and Author

In an old and dying industry in which demand drops, the worst thing to do is to modernize production facilities.

BOARDROOM REPORTS

Fast-growing companies generally run into trouble at about $10 million in sales (when management's needs outstrip the founder's capacity). They run into trouble again at about $40 million in sales, when professional management techniques usually need to be installed.

┌ **Business Rules of Thumb** ┐
└ **HALL OF FAME** ┘

MICHAEL E. PORTER—Mr. Porter is one of the world's leading authorities on business competitive strategies. He is a professor at the Harvard Graduate Business School and the recipient of the McKinsey Foundation Award for the Best Harvard Business School Review article of 1979.

JIM BONDURANT
Network Operations Manager
Computerland

You only have to be 1 percent better than your competition in order to succeed. In the mind of your customer, you'll seem 10 percent better. And, in terms of sales, it's worth 100 percent.

ROBERT BURGELMAN
Professor
Stanford Business School

Never attack a competitor on its geographic home turf, as the competitor will likely resort to goals that are not purely economic.

DANIEL CORBETT
Consultant

A business consultant should never charge for less than half a day of work.

DAVID WEINSTEIN
Professor
Stanford Business School

An increase of 10 percent in market share will lead to an increase of five points in pretax return on investment.

DAVID WEINSTEIN

A company which has high fixed costs and low variable costs (as many Japanese companies do) will be more likely to stress high volume sales and an increasing market share.

JOEL DEAN

Five ways to tell if a product is reaching competitive maturity:

1. Weakening in brand preference
2. Narrowing physical variation among products as the best designs are standardized
3. Entry in force of private-label competitors
4. Market saturation
5. Stabilization of production methods

ROBERT GARDA
Director
McKinsey & Co.

Price increases should be publicized if the company can make a well-reasoned, cost-driven case for the increase.

KATHRYN HARRIGAN and MICHAEL PORTER
Harvard Business Review

Pull out of a declining industry if one or more companies with significant resources are committed to staying in.

JOHN SCHUBERT
Magazine Editor

A consultant should charge at least three times the rate he would expect to receive for comparable full-time work with fringe benefits.

KARL VESPER
Author and Professor of Entrepreneurship

In a company, the cost of administration, overhead, and selling should at least equal that of labor and materials.

MICHAEL PORTER
Professor
Harvard Business School

WILLINGNESS OF COMPETITORS TO BACK DOWN

Preemption will be risky against the following types of competitors:

1. Competitors with goals other than purely economic
2. Competitors for whom this business is a major strategic thrust
3. Competitors who have equal or better staying power, a longer time horizon, or a greater willingness to trade profits for market position

BENJAMIN T. OLDS
Management Consultant
Olds & Roberts, Inc.

A corporation should choose a city for its headquarters which most closely matches the corporate culture.

BILL POLAND
President
Bay West Development

Keep the overhead costs of a cyclical business as low as possible.

MICHAEL PORTER

Market growth tends to be a good proxy for required cash investment.

STEVE BRANDT
Entrepreneur, Author, Professor

Remain doggedly customer-centered.

ROBERT TILLMAN
Director of Marketing
Paradise Systems, Inc.

To compete successfully against IBM, a manufacturer needs to offer the same functionality for at least a 15 percent lower price.

THOMAS PETERS
Coauthor
In Search of Excellence

Don't worry about trends. The biggest successes often lie in redefining dormant businesses.

ROBERT TOWNSEND
Former President, Avis Rent-A-Car
Author, Up the Organization

Build a 20 percent pessimism quotient into all expectations. Overestimate by 20 percent the amount of time it will take to accomplish a plan. Underestimate by 20 percent the expected results.

┌──┐
│ ── **Business Rules of Thumb** ──   │
│ ──── **HALL OF FAME** ────   │
│   │
│ ROBERT TOWNSEND—Mr. Townsend is well known │
│ for his successful tenure as president of Avis Rent-A- │
│ Car, Inc., as well as for his 1970 book, *Up the Or-* │
│ *ganization*. The *New York Times* called him "one of │
│ the most original top executives of the past decade." │
└──┘

MICHAEL PORTER

The three basic strategies to cope with fierce competitive forces are: overall cost leadership, differentiation, and focus.

LEONARD PACE
Management Consultant
Deloitte, Haskins & Sells

If a company has the money, it will be much less expensive to penetrate a new market during a weakening in the economy.

KARL VESPER

A consumer product should sell for four or five times the cost of the manufacturer's labor and materials. A service should sell for at least three times the labor cost to the firm.

MICHAEL PORTER

STRATEGIES FOR ENTERING A NEW MARKET

- Reduce product costs.
- Buy in with a low price.

- Offer a superior product.
- Introduce a marketing innovation.
- Use piggyback distribution (from another business).

JAMES P. MANNELLY
Vice-president
Tenant Co.

Four areas should be regularly checked, both for short-term results (one year or less) and longer-term results: sales volume vs. plan; sales costs; market share vs. competition; and development of salespeople.

HAROLD LEAVITT
Professor
Stanford Business School

The greater the cultural difference between a parent company and its offshoot international organization, the more autonomy the offshoot needs.

MICHAEL PORTER

Conditions that signal the strong likelihood of retaliation to entry and hence deter it are the following:

1. A history of vigorous retaliation to entrants
2. Established firms with substantial resources to fight back
3. Established firms with great commitment to the industry and highly illiquid assets
4. Slow industry growth

JOEL DEAN

What to do if a product reaches maturity:

1. Cut prices when needed.
2. Emphasize product improvements.

DAVID WEINSTEIN

Typically, the higher the capital intensity of an industry or company, the lower the return on investment.

DAVID WEINSTEIN

Market share is more important for infrequently purchased products, as the buyer places a premium on taking less risk in the purchase.

CHIP CONLEY

If you own a company with a partner in which each person must make a critical contribution, make sure you share ownership 50/50.

BOARDROOM REPORTS

Most companies don't establish an international business until their sales reach the $30-to-$50-million level.

18
ANY WAY YOU
FIGURE IT

Finance

MICHAEL BROWN
Principal
Wom Enterprises

In a leveraged buyout, the faster you pay down the debt, the faster you profit.

JAMES C. VAN HORNE
Professor
Stanford Business School

The loser in a leveraged buyout is the employee. The employee takes on more risk and gets the least reward.

CPA CLIENT BULLETIN

An accounts receivable factoring company will typically take a fee equal to 1 percent of your total credit sales plus interest, at 2 or 3 percent above the prime rate, on invoice amounts that are paid before the original due dates.

WILLIAM DAVID MONTAPERT
Author
The Omega Strategy

The future inflation rate is largely determined by the money growth rate prevailing eighteen to twenty-four months previously, minus 1 percent.

FREDERICK T. BALDWIN IV
Stock Analyst

Investment banks tend to have an average return on equity equal to twice that of commercial banks.

DICK BERRY
Industrial Marketing Results

Customer service problems are the cause of 30 percent of the decisions to switch banks.

BOARDROOM REPORTS

You can get greater attention from bankers by arranging visits to coincide with their least busy period. Best times: between the 4th and 14th or between the 16th and 29th of the month. And before 11 A.M. or after 1:30 P.M.

CHIP CONLEY

Don't go before a bank loan committee prior to the Christmas holiday, as it is quite likely you won't get a response until the new year.

GUY C. ROBERTS
Massachusetts Life Insurance Co.

WHAT BANK LOAN OFFICERS LOOK FOR FROM A COMPANY

- A long-term record of solid or expanding market share
- Company finances that emphasize long-term debt
- Return on capital of 8 percent or more
- Use of an independent CPA, preferably one of the Big Eight
- A comprehensive company financial plan

JOHN McDONALD
Professor
Stanford Business School

Companies in high margin businesses tend to be less concerned about collecting accounts receivable on time.

HORACE KLAFTER
Business and Professional Research Institute

Figure to pay 20 to 40 percent of the amount collected to a collection firm.

JOHN McDONALD

If you add new shares to a company, profit must increase by at least the P/E ratio in order to eliminate the potential for stock dilution.

HENRY VOSS
Entrepreneur

Require all department heads to cut at least two percent of their existing annual budget, regardless of new budget items which may be included next year.

CARL OWEN
Investment Banker

Borrow as much as you can, not just what you think you'll need.

SID FEINSTEIN
Floral Executive

Never use the president's or marketing manager's name in correspondence on debt collections with customers.

RICHARD M. WHITE
Author
The Entrepreneur's Manual

Finance salaries should not exceed .5 percent of net sales after the second year.

CHIP CONLEY

The best time to borrow from a bank is when the economy is in an upturn and when banks are in heavy competition with each other.

KARL VESPER
Author and Professor of Entrepreneurship

Goodwill as a percentage of gross sales in the purchase of small businesses:
- Travel agency: 35%
- Small coin-op laundry: 70%
- Accounting practice: 90–150%
- Insurance agency with sales greater than $100,000: 200%
- Large radio station: 600%

RICHARD M. WHITE

PRICE (EARNINGS) RATIOS

- Decaying industry: 2.5 to 5
- Stagnant industry: 4 to 10
- Older growth industry: 7.5 to 25
- Vigorous growth industry: 25 to 75
- Growth and glamour industries: 50 to 1000

ROWENA SCOTT
President
The Scott Group of America

An acquiring corporation typically pays 30 percent over book value of the corporation which they are acquiring.

WILLIAM M. GRAY
Senior Analyst
Goldman, Sachs

A healthy company which is aggressive in dealing with the financial community will have a higher price/earnings ratio than one that is not.

BOB WARRINGTON
Vice-president
Deak-Perera

If you want to save time and money when your business sends payments overseas, pay in local currency, not U.S. dollars.

T. MARTIN and B. TRABUE
Authors
Sell More and Spend Less

Instead of marking the invoice with the standardized code (e.g., 2%/10 net 30), translate the savings into plain English. Sample: This is our offer of 36% interest.

ROBERT TILLMAN
Director of Marketing
Paradise Systems, Inc.

Inexperienced investors (in a company), while they may pay the highest price for the stock, are often the most expensive choice in the long run.

RICHARD M. WHITE

PRIORITIES OF PAYMENTS

1. Pay your banker.
2. Pay other lenders.
3. Pay your workers.
4. Pay your other creditors.
5. Pay yourself.

PHILIP J. FOX and JOSEPH MANCUSO
Authors
402 Things You Should Know Before Starting a New Business

Always give low sales estimates in talking to potential investors or a bank.

PETER DRUCKER
Noted Business Commentator and Author

1. An acquisition will succeed only if the acquiring company thinks through what it can contribute to the business it is buying.
2. Successful diversification by acquisition requires a core of unity. The two businesses must have in common either markets or technology.
3. No acquisition works unless the people in the acquiring company respect the product, the markets, and the customer of the company they acquire.
4. Within a year or so, an acquiring company must be able to provide top management for the company it acquires. It is an elementary fallacy to believe one can "buy" management. The buyer has to be prepared to lose the top incumbents in companies that are bought.
5. Within the first year of a merger, it is important that a large number of people in the management groups of both companies receive substantial promotions across the lines (from one company to another).

MARC J. WALFISH
Regional Vice-president
PruCapital, Inc.

The company arranging a leveraged buyout should be able to pay off between one-third and one-half the resulting debt within a five-year period.

RICHARD M. WHITE

Administration salaries should not exceed 3 percent of net sales after the fifth year.

MICHAEL PORTER
Professor
Harvard Business School

Sustainable growth = (asset growth) × (aftertax return on sales) × (assets/debt) × (debt/equity) × (fraction of earnings retained).

JOHN McDONALD

A company's current ratio ought to be twice the size of its quick ratio.

JAMES WICKER
Partner
Peat Marwick & Mitchell

Stratify suppliers into those that:

- Must be paid currently
- Accept late payment occasionally
- Take late payment as a matter of informal policy

GEORGE FOSTER
Professor
Stanford Business School

A commercial bank should have no more than 5 percent of its lending portfolio in any one industry.

JOHN McDONALD

For every dollar of inventory, a company can collateralize fifty cents of it for a loan. For every dollar of accounts receivable, a company can typically collateralize eighty cents of it for a loan.

BOARDROOM REPORTS

In negotiating a loan with a bank: radiate a sense of confidence, underplay how much the bank needs to know, never give ultimatums, and phrase requests so other parties think they have a choice.

ALEXANDER GRANT & CO.

TABLE OF COLLECTION LIKELIHOOD

30 days	97 cents on the dollar
90 days	90 cents
120 days	80 cents
180 days	67 cents

19
BITS AND BYTES
Computers

BOARDROOM REPORTS

Purchase a new computer if the replacement parts and software to upgrade the old system are more than 50 percent of the original purchase price.

PETER McWILLIAMS
Author
The Personal Computer Book

The causes of costly mistakes, in order, are:

1. Operator error
2. Software error
3. Computer error

Using software and computers that have been around for a while minimizes categories two and three.

DAVE McKEOWN
Computer Scientist

Every two years, you can buy a computer that performs twice as well at half the price.

PETER McWILLIAMS

In a very small company, a personal computer will roughly double the output of a secretary and a bookkeeper.

EDWARD BROOKS

For every two days spent designing a computer system, figure one day for coding or writing the program and three days testing it.

SETH GODIN

Start-up companies are far more likely to have computers than established ones.

PETER McWILLIAMS

TEN RULES FOR BUYING A COMPUTER

1. Make an appointment.
2. Do not be intimidated by jargon.
3. Get some "hands-on" experience—try it out.
4. Ask a friend who knows something about computers to come along.
5. Use the computer for what you'll be using the computer for.
6. Be on the lookout for good salespeople as well as good computers.
7. Make notes.
8. Trust your intuition.
9. Investigate the warranty.
10. Take your time.

J. RICHARD FLEMING
Principal
System Planning Associates

Putting a company on-line takes six to nine months of preparation, conversion, and integration. Then it takes another three to six months to fully absorb changes and to reap the revised systems benefits.

ROBERT PURSER
Telocator Corp.

Word processors are least valuable for fast typists who make fewer than three errors per page.

THE BUSINESS AUTOMATION BULLETIN

A computer system capable of doing record keeping and accounting for a business should cost 1 to 2 percent of the company's annual sales.

J. RICHARD FLEMING

A company should not computerize order entry, fulfillment, billing, accounts receivable, credit commissions accounting, or sales analysis in a piecemeal fashion.

CHIP CONLEY

Computer companies (and accountants) are twice as likely as other companies to occupy office space in a building with locked bathrooms (the kind that you need a key to get into).

WILLIAM STEINBERGER
Control Data Corp.

Be careful about putting a programmer in charge of the data processing department. They commonly expand the role of the computer beyond the company's needs.

ROBERT LONDON
Brandon Consulting

A company's equipment and programming needs double within two years of computer purchase.

J. RICHARD FLEMING

A company will realize the biggest single payback by computerizing its entire sales order processing.

INFOWORLD

The productivity of a company's programming staff is directly proportional to the quantity and variety of junk food available.

DICK BRATT
Vice-president, Engineering
Spinnaker Software

A good programmer can create one thousand lines of debugged code per year, regardless of the computer language being used.

CLIFTON ROYSTON
Programmer/Analyst

Making a design change when a computer system is nearly complete will cost about ten times as much as making the change before the work has started.

20

MAKING WIDGETS
Production and Line Operations

JONN MITCHELL
President
Motorola

A manufacturing or R&D plant should never allow its employment level to exceed one thousand people.

TOM PETERS and BOB WATERMAN
Authors
In Search of Excellence

If you assemble more than seven people on a research project, you can be assured that research effectiveness will decrease.

BOARDROOM REPORTS

Locate managers' offices in the center of the plant so that production workers can have easy access to them, without having to go through an intermediary.

DAVID KREPS
Professor
Stanford Business School

The amount of inventory a company stores should be proportional to how critical the resource is which develops that inventory.

JOHN DAVIN
Vice-president, Materials and Facilities
GTE Service Co.

What to do as soon as sales fall short of projections:

1. Communicate the information as fast as possible to production and purchasing managers.
2. Build in the financial controls necessary to trigger a purchasing alert. Delay means a continuing buildup of raw materials and finished products for which there are no ready buyers.

DR. JOSEPH JURUM
Quality Control Consultant

One-third of all quality-control problems originate in the product's design. One-half result from flaws in purchased components.

LYNN PHILLIPS
Professor
Stanford Business School

The amount of purchases from a company's top two material suppliers should be no greater than 60 percent of all purchases and should be divided equally between the two.

JACK LINDSAY
Energy User News

Skylights can save 80 to 90 percent of lighting energy during daylight hours.

PHILIP J. FOX and JOSEPH R. MANCUSO
Authors
402 Things You Should Know Before Starting a New Business

In calculating rough costs for a product made overseas, add 20 percent to the cost of the product when it leaves the plant, wherever that is.

RAY BRUMAN

The materials for a mass-produced electronic device should cost about 10 percent of the retail price of the finished product.

RICHARD M. WHITE
Author
The Entrepreneur's Manual

The materials purchased in a manufacturing start-up should not exceed 10 percent of net sales.

SELWIN E. PRICE
Partner
Alexander Grant & Co.

It costs twenty to twenty-five cents to carry one dollar's worth of unsold inventory for a year (fifteen cents for interest, eight cents for space, handling, utilities, and insurance).

U.S. DEPARTMENT OF AGRICULTURE

Packaging cost for food and beverages is about 9 percent of total cost.

TOM PETERS
Coauthor
In Search of Excellence

If you are serious about product quality/customer service, and you're not spending 35 percent of your time on it (by gross calendar analysis), then you are not serious about it.

RICHARD M. WHITE

R&D budgets shouldn't drop too far below 10 percent in a manufacturing start-up or 15 percent in a high-tech start-up.

PHILIP J. FOX and JOSEPH R. MANCUSO

Require price quotes from three different suppliers when purchasing raw materials for production.

PETERSON, HOWELL & HEATHER
Transportation Consultants

Replace fleet cars at thirty-six months or 55,000 miles. This is the point when the cost of keeping the car exceeds the cost of a new one.

RICHARD M. WHITE

In manufacturing companies, the production salaries shouldn't exceed 15 percent of net sales.

NORMAN KOBERT
Inventory Consultant

Always expand upward where possible—it saves rent dollars.

DR. DOUGLAS LAMBERT
Michigan State Business School

Keep inventory turns to five or six a year for maximum cost efficiency.

JOHN O'CONNOR
Editorial Director
Purchasing Magazine

Firms tend to change 20 to 25 percent of their suppliers annually.

JOHN CHRISTIANSON
Manufacturing Specialist

Production costs shouldn't exceed 10 percent of sales price in the start-up phase of a manufacturing firm.

DAVID KREPS

The bigger the capacity difference between production stations, the larger the inventory which needs to be held.

CYNTHIA ORR
Consulting Geophysicist

As a rule, 20 percent of a product line produces 80 percent of the profit.

GEORGE BALLAS and DAVID HOLLAS
Authors
Making of an Entrepreneuer

Companies in a growth industry should buy rather than make component parts.

21
THE TAO JONES INDEX
Business Philosophy

ROGER VON OECH
Author
A Whack on the Side of the Head

The amount a person uses his imagination is inversely proportional to the amount of punishment he will receive for using it.

JOHN OPEL
Chairman of the Board
IBM

Be scrupulously honest.
Figure out what creates utility in your job.
Associate yourself with quality people.

NAPOLEON HILL
Author
Think and Grow Rich

NAPOLEON HILL'S 13 PRINCIPLES FOR SUCCESS

1. Desire
2. Faith
3. Autosuggestion
4. Specialized knowledge
5. Imagination
6. Organized planning
7. Decision-making ability
8. Persistence
9. Power of the Master Mind—use of a business support group
10. Sex transmutation
11. Subconscious mind
12. Brain utilization
13. The sixth sense

LAURENCE J. PETER
Author
The Peter Principle

Everyone is promoted to their level of incompetence.

Business Rules of Thumb
HALL OF FAME

DR. LAURENCE J. PETER—Dr. Peter has devoted his life to discovering remedies for incompetence and is widely known for his development of systems for improvement of education. The Peter Principle, "In a hierarchy, every employee tends to rise to his level of incompetence," is one of the best-known rules ever established.

CHIP CONLEY

The frequency and length of an executive's career sabbatical are directly proportional to the number of hours the executive works per week.

ROGER VON OECH

Almost every advance in art, science, technology, business, marketing, cooking, medicine, agriculture, and design has occurred when someone challenged the rules and tried another approach.

PETER DRUCKER
Noted Business Commentator and Author

The distance between the leaders and the average is a constant. If leadership performance is high, the average will go up. It is easier to raise the performance of one leader than it is to raise the performance of a whole mass.

FREDERICK TERMAN (THE FATHER OF SILICON VALLEY)
Former Provost
Stanford University

If you want a track team to win the high jump, you find one person who can jump seven feet, not seven people who can jump one foot.

C. NORTHCOTE PARKINSON
Noted Business Commentator

Work expands so as to fill the time available for its completion.

CHIP CONLEY

The success of a chief executive officer is directly proportional to the length of time he has worked with his executive secretary.

DALE CARNEGIE
Noted Author and Philosopher

A man convinced against his will is of the same opinion still.

KEVIN O'BEIRNE
Mortgage Broker

Beware of people who abbreviate their first name to an initial (e.g., J. Edgar Hoover).

PETER DRUCKER

The effective executive asks, "What results are expected of me?" rather than, "What work needs to be done?"

CHIP CONLEY

Executives who are only children or firstborns are twice as likely to succeed as middle children or latter-borns.

SETH GODIN

Learn to handle rejection. It's easy to handle success.

AL RIES and JACK TROUT
Authors
Positioning: The Battle for Your Mind

Cherchez le créneau—find a hole then fill it.

WOODY ALLEN
Comedian

Eighty percent of success is showing up.

MARK JOHNSON
Art Entrepreneur

To be masterful at anything, you must be completely reckless, and make lots of mistakes—big ones!

DAVID OGILVY
Founder
Ogilvy & Mather

Rules are for the obedience of fools and the guidance of wise men.